Measuring Impact of Diabetes On Quality of Life

Bharti, Ashok Kumar

Acknowledgements

I owe a huge of gratitude to my esteemed guide Dr. Namita Gupta, Dean Faculty of Social Science & Head, University Department of Psychology, Vinoba Bhave University, Hazaribagh, for her guidance throughout the journey of my research with extensive knowledge, research experience invaluable suggestions and the most importantly co-operation, and immense patience at every step. I feel fortunate enough to get the chance to work with her.

I express my sincere gratitude Dr. Sadique Razaque, Ex Head, University Department of Psychology, Vinoba Bhave University, Hazaribagh, Dr. Avinash Kumar Singh, Assistant Professor, University Department of Psychology, Vinoba Bhave University, Hazaribagh and Dr. Vijay Kumar. I warmly thank to them for their valuable advice, constructive criticism and their extensive discussion during my research work.

Results described in this thesis would have not been gained without a response of diabetic and non-diabetic subjects. Therefore my acknowledgement goes to all respondents who made the difficult task of data collection possible for my research.

I am thankful to my parents, family and friends too, who helped and supported for the completion of my research study.

Finally I would like to thank the Almighty God for blessing, who gave me the strength to do the hard work throughout this research work.

CONTENTS

Chapter-1

Chapter-2

Chapter-3

Chapter-4

Chapter-5

LIST OF FIGURES

LIST OF TABLES

CHAPTER – 1

INTRODUCTION

LIST OF CONTENTS

Chapter-1

1 Introduction

Diabetes a silently killing, currently it is doing billions of dollars of harm to our society, which involves a large amount of innocent citizens oncology patients and millions of others. either as a Type 1 diabetes is long-where the pancreas stops producing insulin or as a result of the patient's body not being able to access the insulin — in a severe long-term illness or all of diabetes — Type 1 diabetes is possible There is growing evidence that suggests a link between lifestyle and rising diabetes rates in the world of the 21st century, but rising levels of obesity are not considered one of equal importance with that of identifying the disease as a global health crisis. As the condition has been described, diabetes is something that develops over time; it takes several alterations in lifestyle to treat and is called the most demanding of all chronic diseases.

Diabetes must be closely controlled by taking medication and exercising every day, because the only way to treat it is to use any of it must be avoided. Because people who suffer from this disorder must undergo dietary adjustments and sometimes struggle with anxiety difficulties, the odds of them having several health conditions are higher. Individuals that are obese are less likely to be satisfied with their lives and are therefore more likely to engage in negative habits including smoking and alcohol and are physically inactive are more likely to be dissatisfied. The new style of life which is prevalent in the world's largest cities and has since been incorporated into the developing cities and metros has been referred to as the global style of urban life, while citizens all of the above cities/cities adhere to this today have only to a portion of its features.

Unfortunately, diabetes has a major impact on the life of many people, and the possibility that people with diabetes can have a worse quality of life is enough for others to consider preventing it when such long-term diseases such as obesity, sleep apnea, heart disease, and kidney disease coexist with diabetes, their symptoms are intensified. Owing to developing diabetes, there is an approximately twofold rise in the chances of fear, shifts in diet, and other challenges twice the chance of marriage issues. In order to survive, people must detect the danger and avoid or decline into a state of unawareness. Under that scenario, the body's anatomy is greatly expands. Problems follow, and certain essential organs are impacted. There is a significant disparity between the demands and the country has on the three relevant to science, schooling, and health care, for Indian citizens for additional treatment.

1.2 Concept of Diabetes

Many people who are going blind, in part due to diabetes, billions who have lost their sight due to diabetes around the world today are in addition to a potentially deadly illness. Often, people who have the illness of job burn will go through all the physical symptoms of cancer before being diagnosed. In these cases, job burn is as fatal as the disease if not identified. Gelatinous retinopathy, formerly known as retinopathy of gelatinous, is an exceedingly common condition that usually causes severe vision loss in both eyes and an unusually rapid breakdown of the skin and blood vessels. Diabetes is a lack of self-control over insulin levels, which is marked by a syphon. There is another expression that describes diabetes, "non-insulin-dependent" or "no-need-for-for-insulin-sugar diabetes". "Non-insulin-dependent" describes it as the disease of having the property of becoming nondiabetic under which the urine is free of sugar. There was the first known account of diabetes, which appeared in 1550 B.C.C. It tells about a condition that led a patient to lose weight easily and regularly as well as having trouble urinating. Diabetes has been perceived for 2,000 years as a lethal and crippling illness for the past 2,000 years. Diabetes, also being a form a Greek word meaning "to destroy", was given the Latin name "sus" (or Cynic form of it) after its discoverer, "Aretaeus, and referred to as a disease which degrades the patient's entire body over time. For fluids linger in the body just to get from place to place; they never carry it for their final dwelling. An average human lifetime may be roughly a century, say, but not usually, decades long. Though it can be excruciating for them, they stand beside you, urination is also easy. Because no vital component of the drink is consumed, the fluid is mostly consists of flesh, much of the drink is eliminated in the urine.

1.2.1 Types of Diabetes

World Health Organization, an organ of UNO, had pointed out that diabetes mellitus can be classified as for clinical convenience.

(a) Insulin - dependent diabetes mellitus (IDDM).

(b) Non-insulin - dependent diabetes mellitus (NIDDM).

(c) Male-nutrition - related diabetes mellitus (MRDM).

Besides, there are some cases which fall under risk factor. They are subject to normal glucose tolerance but have as increased risk of developing that disease.

(a) Insulin - dependent diabetes mellitus (IDDM) -Insulin output is rather insufficient or zero in certain cases, usually less than 50 years old and less than average or normal weight. These situations involve doses of insulin or external insulin supplementation. Suddenly the woman begins to feel hungry, undergoes excessive urination, has painful muscles, begins to lose weight, and has scratching on her body and her vision blurs. This condition is also prey to infants and young adults.

However, there tend to be no other signs and the patient either goes into a coma or dies. This is really risky and requires medication or oral anti-diabetic drugs urgently. Ketoacidosis that may prove lethal can occur in the patient. Substances like these are prescribed for weight-preserving caloric foods and for insulin injections to retain the necessary blood sugar level. Insulin output is low to non-existent, which results in insulin injections being required everyday. It starts easily. When insulin doses are stopped, the symptoms become extreme. The diabetic produces a life - dangerous metabolism called ketoacidosis. Type 1 diabetes is a condition that primarily impacts adolescents and teens. A steady increase in the blood sugar, which often contributes to symptoms such as severe thirst, repeated urination, weight loss and drowsiness, can go so far as a coma and die without medication, is often called mellitus diabetes. Mellitus diabetes the signs revealed are stronger, the mind is not altered. This type of diabetics plays an important role in the emotional, behavioral, employment and social functioning of people and of their families (Ventura et al. 2019).

(b) Non-insulin - dependent diabetes mellitus (NIDDM)-Patients of this classification have no need for the use of insulin to keep it under control. For the most part, people in the center of their lives become victims, but fewer than 40 might be spared. It seems to have developed steadily and can be spotted with a regular physical examination in certain circumstances, diabetes may be managed with just dietary intervention, including by using oral hypoglycemic medications. They can take their medication on a daily basis. There's nothing more about it. We mustn't offer him an injection of medicine; it will make him - again. Like it or not, it or not, it must be done every quarter. Do not hesitate taking the drug. Doing this is really harmful. Based on the condition and the weight of the patient, medications and diets differ Reducing weight is completely important. You must watch your food consumption while staying nourishing and healthy with your diet. There are two types of diabetes; insulin-dependent diabetes and non-insulin-dependent diabetes. They can be fully regulated by means other than surgery, and is just the "not injurious to the body" diabetes or Diabetes mellitus "Totally dependent on insulin", which is also known as "non-allergic" is controlled by means other than that, called "N.I.D." (World Health Organization, 1999; ADA, 2009b). And for all of the advances in research, the amount of individuals afflicted by type 2 diabetes is also increasing as well as the socio-economic consequences due to the management and complications of the condition.

(c) Malnutrition - related diabetes mellitus (MRDM) -People who are afflicted with diabetes and have suffered under more stress in warmer, developing countries display symptoms of malnutrition and other health problems, according to a World Health Organization (WHO) study They are often listed as having Insulin - dependent diabetes mellitus (IDDM)and Non-insulin - dependent diabetes mellitus (NIDDM)are put here. While tropical areas such as the Americas, India, Bangladesh, Africa, Kenya, Nigeria, and Uganda are notorious for their case load of poverty, there are alldispover organizations under which wealth is equally redistributed among the population.

1.2.2 Causes of the rise in Prevalence of Diabetes

Type II Diabetes Mellitus as a common and complex disease has been characterized by the following causes:

(a) Obesity – Obesity is a significant risk factor for developing type 2 diabetes. The association between greater weight gain and elevated diabetes risk is more pronounced in Asian cultures, thereby needing a lower body mass index cut-off value to accurately classify individuals. To increase their chance of cardiovascular wellbeing, Indian men should have a body mass index of 23 kg, while women should be less than the value for which 82.2 at the waist. The body mass index (BMI) cut-for-cut off point for Indians is 23 kg/m for men and women should be lower than this value, which is 82 cm around the waist.

(b) Abdominal - The amount of general adiposity is variable among Indians, with some seeming to be more than others, but the fat around the abdomen is markedly more prevalent.

(c) Imbalance - Human physiology is out of whack. Changes in job habits from hard to sedentary work, as well as urbanization, mechanization, and increased transportation, have had an effect on human metabolism, and has been related to type 2 diabetes.

(d) Genes - Since 2007, about 20 genes (such as TCF7L2, HHEX, CDKAL1, SLC30A8, and others) have been linked to type 2 diabetes mellitus in genome-wide association studies (odds ratios varying from 1.2 to 1.5).

(e) Ethnicity - While factors including increased environmental factors and genetic variance and/insulin tolerance in the reduced a differential in European, Asian populations have both contribute to Asian Indian peoples' propensity to diabetes, in type 2 diabetes the environmental/gene influences have a lot more variety contributes to the whole-Specificity is definitely responsible for this phenomenon. Other variables in major acquired status include a sedentary lifestyle (which includes not exercising) and diets high in animal products. Also, as all ethnic groups are affected by insulin resistance, factors including age are causes, here is being mentioned.

(f) Early life - Development in the likelihood of diabetes: having a small uterus or getting growth spurt in early adolescence could both have an effect on risk effect on the chance of complications including artery disease. Babies in the weigh less at birth and are more frequently placed at risk of diabetes and the metabolic syndrome as they age in the Indian population in rural areas because of the under nutrition of their mothers during pregnancy. This class is designed for persons who have excess body fat as a few weeks before birth, as well as for those who are born at a moderate weight.

(g) Low level of awareness - Furthermore, citizens residing in rural areas are less conscious of the problems as opposed to people in the towns, and this reality compounds the problem.

1.2.3 Delay of Type II Diabetes

They would have 'almost always' be identified as having Type 2 diabetes due to the advent of type 2 diabetes because of "abnormal "pre-diabetes" blood glucose levels that has risen. Diabetes is a life-threatening disease that must be attended to immediately if it is detected early. This recently performed research proves that people with pre diabetes can postpone or delay the onset of type 2 diabetes by making lifestyle improvements, including increasing physical activity. Additionally, the ability for them to get their blood glucose levels back to normal could be understood. changes in one's lifestyle are the most significant There is data to support a combination of the hypothesis that a diet and an improvement in physical exercise will assist with healthy weight, aid with longer lasting wellbeing, and lower the risk of diabetes. The findings of the Diabetes Prevention Study (DP) demonstrated that weight loss by a well- and activity moderate exercise could decrease or postpone the risk of developing Type II diabetes.

1.2.4 Risk Factors

Any risk factors correlated with diabetes are something that we can manage, such as obesity and sedentary habits. Nonetheless, causes such as ancestry and inheritance are considerable sources of concern for illness, even if they cannot be prevented. Type I diabetes is a genetic, chronic disorder that is directly related to the following a family history of the disease. It is an important risk factor if the family has a history of diabetes. The American Diabetes Association advises individuals with one or more first-degree relatives who are prone to develop diabetes – a mother, father, brother, or sister with Type I diabetes, for example– to undergo testing for diabetes. It is possible to detect Type I diabetes with a clear blood examination. People who have Type I diabetes have often had the additional issue of accidents or disorders of the pan creaseprain impeding insulin development. Type I diabetes. One of the conditions which can induce diabetes is a spectrum of infections and illnesses that targets the pancreas (Laakso, 1999).

Type II diabetes has a risk factors that include: being overweight, being inactive, and insulin tolerance, having a family history of the disease, and inherited traits, plus heredity and heritage all contribute to raising the chances of being afflicted. Concerns having to do with biology have demonstrated that there are many hereditary differences that may increase the likelihood of diabetes development the same genes are seen in the tissues of the body, as well as reduced insulin release, which is another way of saying that they are found to be linked with obesity. Such as native Hawaiians, however higher levels of diabetes in other racial groups such as African Americans, American Indians, Native Hawaiians, and other indigenous people of the Pacific Islanders, and other indigenous Pacific Islanders such as Mexican Americans In addition to this, the classes mentioned above, there is an elevated likelihood of both diabetes and cardiac disease. It's not only because of the increase in hypertension, obesity, and type 2 diabetes in these groups, but also to smaller blood volumes and lower dietary and activity levels are also. In comparison, among African Americans, it is more popular to find the sort of diabetes recognized as "Type II" than "a European," and thus more individuals have this form of the disorder than the illness (Boulton et. al., 2005).While being known to be important risk factors, they are not the only causes of diabetes; often, race and genes are linked to who you became a diabetic.

Diets that have shifted and the path and fitness levels that are linked to recent urbanization and technical developments have undergone sharp changes as a significant factors have contributed to diabetes rises. Diabetes was seen to have a statistical correlation with the background of alcohol usage of use in patients known to have developed at a younger age. An inquiry undertaken in the US finds that opioid usage had been linked to it, according to studies in the States (Karlon et. al., 2001). Marijuana and cocaine are the most commonly used illegal substances, although there are several others as well.

1.2.5 Diet and Diabetes Mellitus

Sedentary behavior and overeating, which leads to obesity, are two main environmental causes that contribute to type 2 diabetes in urbanized communities, sedentary behavior is more normal.

Dietary advice is essential upon diagnosis of diabetes. Normal advice includes:

- reducing intake of fatty foods eating mainly vegetables, fruit, cereal, rice and pasta (using whole meal products where possible)
- eating only small amounts of refined sugar (jam, sweets etc.)
- eating at regular intervals
- carrying glucose tablets, sweets or products in case of hypoglycemia
- exercising regularly; not only does it helps reduce hyperglycemia, but it also reduces insulin resistance by reducing obesity.

It's in most situations avoidable, whether you make smart lifestyle adjustments, but in others it is potentially reversible. If you are thinking about action to avoid or regulate diabetes, yours not thinking about going without food. Patients don't have to give up their favorite foods or forgo all desserts for the rest of their lives if they choose to eat healthier, so they should take steps to include enjoying more and/overcoming their candy cravings. You can consume carbohydrates which have a stronger effect on your blood sugar levels than you can for any fats or proteins. Patients can usually obey a high-up the following nutritional instructions: Exclude extremely processed carbs including white bread, pasta, sugar, and rice, and snack items. Instead of focusing on quick, short-acting carbs, look at higher- fiber, low-residue carbs, known as slower-acting carbs. Carbs that are low in glycemic and are slowly digested are better for people with diabetes since they are less prone to increase blood sugar levels than rapid-digested carbs. They are often helpful for people because they have a steady supply of energy but make people remain complete for a longer period of time.

1.2.6 Exercise and Diabetes Mellitus

Reasonable physical exercise decreases the risk of type II diabetes by at least 30% per day will reduce it by at least 30%. Diabetes has an opposite relationship with physical activity: the less the workout you perform, the greater the risk will be (Gkaliagkousi 2007). Regular activity has positive impact on glycemic regulation across both cases of diabetes. T2D is the key contributor to glycemia (low blood sugar), and physical activity is the most effective way to diminish glymic tolerance (maintaining the usual blood sugar level). The several aspects in which physical exercise promotes insulin sensitivity including decreasing insulin resistance. A significant contribution to insulin resistance develops because of fat production in the liver. As exercise increases the body's use of insulin and decreases free fatty acid levels in the blood. Research has shown that physical activity helps to lower the fatty acid levels in the blood and this way and minimize hepatic insulin resistance (Haus et. al., 2010).

The public health guidance released a suggestion to work up to at least 30 minutes a day or participate in 150 minutes of moderate exercise per week to boost your stamina and general performance (in partnership with doctors) (Tuomileh& coauthors 2001) (Diabetes Prevention Programme research group in NEJM 2002). Protective factors involve weight loss, which can help to avoid the metabolic syndrome's underlying complications including hypertension, lipid defects, and inflammatory markers, as well as vessel functioning improvement; in addition, obesity or the observed/potential for becoming a risk factor may also poses various other side effects including liver fat deposition, atherosclerosis, and probably inflammation (Gkliagkousi 2007).

As those that engage in regular physical activity will quickly find, a positive impact on their mood and physical discomfort, and the restoration, as a greater sense of well-being, individuals who are anxious or depressed will see that they receive more rest while they work out. Strengthening and vigorous exercise allows individuals, regardless of age, sex, and everyone who engages in moderate-to-intensity physical exercises to remain stable and strong and enhance bone and muscle strength (American Diabetes Association: Standards of medical care in diabetes-2007).

1.2.7 Psychological Factors and Diabetes Mellitus

Any possibly fatal illness has severe repercussions for a person's psychological well-being, as well as physical health. At the start, the family may likely be filled with frustration and rejection, however in Type 1 diabetes, participants may move to negotiation and sadness, before ultimately giving in and accepting the situation. In general, concern, the increase in people's awareness and knowledge of the importance of behavioral and emotional causes in the patients' lives is a good thing, as well as in particular for those with diabetes (Glasgow et. al., 1999). There is little discussion on whether diabetes has an impact on quality of life, and whether it is reason for concern. This begs the issue of whether a patient motivation or motivation in regard to diabetes plays a part in self-management. According to experts, diabetes has developed as a key player because of how important it is for quality of health. This broad study is done to seek quality answers to these new questions. Other than on people's wellbeing, including social reinforcement, coping styles, personality traits, and an individual's perspective on life can be a factor in the amount of quality of life a person gets. It is probable that diabetes can exerts an impact in an either immediate or indirect way on the ill effects on the case.

People's social interactions remain strong predictors of quality of life, despite having been dominated by important medical problems, which may differ greatly from individual to person to person, so to a complicated (Peyrot et. al., 1999). higher levels of social care, wages, an individual has, lower instances of physical inactivity, and less medical and mental complications, or self- such as: quality of life in adults has recently been connected to more daily or frequent use of the walking, greater regular social support, educational, and occupational, and an absence of severe disease, less physical inactivity, less impairment in bodily functions and feeling their overall well-being, and emotional condition, as well as financial well (Aalto et. al., 1997).

1.2.8 Specific Psychological Problems in Diabetes

- **Fear of hypoglycemia** - The subjectively uncomfortable experience of hypoglycemia can trigger the person to be so anxious to prevent its recurrence that they run their blood glucose far higher than recommended (especially at night), and glycemic control deteriorates as a consequence.
- **Acceptance of diagnosis, denial and uncertainty** - Patients that have obtained a new diagnosis of diabetes identify the challenges that arise from the diagnosis of the condition often also, they could be reporting trouble recognizing the evaluation of a long-term problem involving long stretches of self-manageable screech. Depression and grief can result in several of course in poor regulation of blood sugar levels, ranging from simple denial of it to refusal to investigate to self-suppressing symptoms to hidden depressed symptoms to complex hyperactivity or denial of an associated grief.
- **Fear of complications** - Although most patients will place themselves in the frame of mind of the likely future harmful consequences of a treatment, there is also a limited percentage of individuals who dread it and become apprehensive of becoming sick. Her/his/his initiative has been fruitless in attempting to regulate her/his diabetes is the fact that he/she sees an elevated blood glucose levels because of it. She/he believes, "no matter what," that she/he may have more problems arising from it. If an individual thinks they are doing what they should be doing is making the condition harder, they are less inclined to follow proper diabetes prevention methods, which paradoxically can raise the likelihood of complications.

Adherence - Adherence to the self-care routine is also hindering diabetes management. This may be for any of several causes, including concentration issues. There are so many expectations of self-management that they sometimes cannot be accommodated in hectic schedules. These critical activities must be prioritized by the user, to happen. The vast majority of those who have diabetes realize what they can do to treat their condition, but everyday life becomes an obstacle.

1.3 Concept of Quality of Life

"Having a decent quality of life" is now seen as a significant, on its own, as well as a prerequisite of good health measures. The word "health" did not only signify absence of sickness and dependency, but also includes factors such as physical, emotional, and social. This was reported more than 70 years earlier by the World Health Organization (World Health Organization: Handbook of Basic Documents 1952). Diabetics agree that good health treatment doesn't end with better health; it includes improved quality of living, mental well-being, and physical and social well-being, as well.

Diabetes is a severe, ongoing challenge, particularly as we get older. So many Diabetics say that diabetes does have a strong impact on their life and that most of them feel burdened by its complications, so they describe it as "hypodermic stress." The acute or long-term stress of hypoglycemia, and the persistent stress of diabetes-related complications can be more challenging, making all of these conditions much more emotionally and socially stressful

There is no dispute that diabetes has a negative impact on quality of life. The quality of life is a three-dimensional concept which includes one which incorporates both the individual's subjective sense of physical, emotional, which social well-being, and includes cognitive (happiness) (Richard 2000). It is really necessary for patients with diabetes and their providers to know their quality of life, because it impacts their well-being, although for various purposes. Hypoglycemia may contribute to a larger decline in self-care, which in turn results in a rise in symptoms and worsening of the condition.

Much as in the general population, some socioeconomic factors are linked to having a high standard of life for diabetics as well:

- On average, men experience a greater sense of well-being than women.
- In general, citizens perceive that the standard of life of younger generations is greater than that of the older ones.
- The further schooling or money an individual has, the greater his or her quality of life.

The quality of life, especially in the type of life which men with diabetes lead, is something that should be given additional attention for men with diabetes. The sex drives of both men and women may be damaged by nerve injury and small vessel disease, but women's symptoms are usually gone undetected before the condition becomes even more serious. Furthermore, the National Diabetes Information Center (ND) estimates that 20% to 75% of men who have diabetes still suffer from erectile dysfunction(www.diabetes.about.com). It is therefore not unusual for men to undergo premature ejaculation.

Most individuals may have age-related changes in their sexual function, whether they want it or not. Diabetes will start impacting men faster and exacerbate their symptoms when a larger amount of their blood and nerve tissue is compromised by their early and/ is diabetic vasculature or nerve problems manifesting in earlier and more seriously in men. When there is no known medical history of diabetes, difficulties will occur about 10-15 years sooner in men than in women. A psychiatrist can even give a recommendation as to a patient with sexual impotence problems; the first move is to indulge in emotional and therapeutic therapy, so to which patients are advised to search out the therapeutic and functional help.

1.3.1 Quality of Life Domains

The main issue for people in general is having the highest possible quality of life. It makes me proud and fulfilled to know that I've done my job and in addition, there is another explanation as well. The consistency of our existence may often take a toll on our wellbeing, and has its own effect on the total quantity. When we are in a good mood, we prefer to take better care of our diabetes; and while we take better care of our diabetes, we remain safe in the long term. Bettering both physically and mentally helps us cope with stress, which helps us live a more fulfilled existence. When you have a decent standard of life, you would definitely continue to expand it and if it expands. Those places of life where the citizenry can actively enjoy high-level living conditions and quality are sometimes referred to as "states of well-being." These fields of study involve subjects include the subjective and the empirical. Regarding quality of life, it, it is important to consider: physical capacity (having the opportunity to carry out physical activities), occupational ability (being able to play vital roles), personal convictions and expectations about the quality of life (which are the product of incorporation of knowledge and feelings regarding and medical problems and how one thinks about their own wellbeing and well-being), and principles about social experiences (which decide personal appraisal of a thoughts on health, which is then informed by what one learns from the family and medical community) Overall well-being, described as the question of how the person communicates with others, the response to him, and with regard to him, and also with social institutions and norms.

The research covers the body's state of health (measured by examinations or assessments performed in a laboratory), as well as other relevant topics such as economy and social support (number and quality of the contacts). 8 cultures have investigated quality of life and determined that it includes the realms of security, stability, economic well-being, access to resources, good health, empowerment, control over family, ability to influence others, and structure, and confidence These eight areas describe a person's degree of personal growth and social integration, as well as well as physical and material well-being.

1.3.2 The Effect of Type 2 Diabetes Mellitus on Quality of Life

Diabetes can often adversely impact the patients' ability to perform in three ways, these categories: quality of life, by keeping them from functioning and living a regular life, by being a factor in their everyday lives, as well as in relationships with relatives, and social life.

In specific, people with long-term illnesses, high levels of living are concerned with quality of life. Type 2 diabetes also has short-term and long-term problems. It often affects well-being and the patient's health condition and quality of life. Since the study concluded that there was an overall difference in the degree of illness between the people with and those without the disease, most stated in terms of living and well-being, more patients, it seems that those with diabetes have worse quality of life. 3 main ways diabetes causes a decline in overall physical health: 1) decreasing sensitivity to insulin, which results in many little ability to fight infections, causing greater mortality in the patient; 2) overwhelming pancreatic hormones, resulting in a greater risk of diabetes-related problems; and eventual deaths; and 3) the sheer destruction of major organs, as a diabetic organs will cause. One of the first problems to arise in patients with diabetes is symptoms that last over lengthy periods of time. This is likely to result in considerable loss of quality of life if a patient results from either of heart failure, impairment of vision, lack of kidneys, debilitating discomfort, and an inability to walk due to paralysis, and the patient's reduced renal capacity, or even though it might not be attributed to their original causes, as well as a severe impairment of both physical and mental (the ability to achieve erections or orgasm). This patient may be incapable of functioning in the home or of performing menial labour, or unwilling to finish ordinary tasks, and will engage in or at a lowered intensity of chores and fun events. It is possible that the patient's capacity to live peacefully will be affected.

There are two important factors to consider. The first is long-term problems, and the second is short- high blood glucose levels may increase overall exhaustion, result in insomnia, and increase the risk of more frequent infections, and lead to more problems, particularly those encountered in immune suppressed individuals There are third causes that affect physical conditions and behavioral adjustments such as elevated carbohydrate requirements owing to the recovery program and issues linked to the person's changed lifestyle. When people must modify their behaviors to control their disease, they are not only facing quality of health problems, but it may even have an impact on their quality of life. there are long-term symptoms of specific anti-diabetic drugs and can often involve gastrointestinal problems such as chronic diarrhea and rosaceous, which is usually induced by another disease named leg thyroid (or type) attributable to injections may also, can often be triggered by the side effects of other than sugar loss for older persons with the possibility of lack of control over both their cognition and their mobility may be more direct than for anxiety over the early onset of health problems related to the latter is more prevalent.

1.4 Concept of Mental Health

It is vital to everyone's well-being to have good health. To be well, having a positive outlook and to start with is essential, but having an optimistic outlook is just further enhancing one's wellbeing when an individual is well, they have the greatest potential for accumulating money. And there is nothing which couldn't be accomplished with a well-functioning mind and a well-functioning body, the human being can do everything. Some people claim that the term wellbeing has various uses for the same idea. For certain individuals, that actually implies they no longer have some sickness or diseases. For others, though, it means being free of any ailments that can be noticed and some, being disease free in everything together. for a psychologist, natural mental wellbeing is to have a balanced thoughts and emotions For a surgeon, it is the main duty of the body to carry out its usual functions Their own approach to the overall well-being, beliefs regarding disease, and their views about the connection between behaviors and behaviour define their own wellbeing in the eyes of the individual.

Physical fitness is one of the most significant aspects of a healthy lifestyle. Unfortunately, there are also so many individuals who are unaware about mental health. A subjective concept like mental wellbeing, such as healthiness is impossible to describe, yet an objective quality such as having an obvious physicality may be found. When we discover insecurity, when we do not know as well as most, we don't worry about it because we expect it to pose new challenges in the process of discovering further information. Clinical practice and study in the behavioral wellbeing sector is extremely critical. Any diseases may be treated with quick tips about how to doings things like exercising and eating healthier habits. There is advice only for people specialized in either malaria or cholera, who advises you to boil water, or swallow drugs that have been sprinkled in filthy water or fail to absorb filthy substances. It is easier to advice for those who are depressed than others who have emotional issues to deal with, as opposed to others who have all kinds of difficulties. Anything they offer can either be general training, or personalized medication, because it doesn't work well. Beliefs and ideas that have been old for ages will impede a specialist's progress. Mental well-being is strongly correlates with physical well-being. Physical fitness and emotional health are interdependent, and must be maintained together. Being mentally well, fulfillment, and peace of mind all have to do with each other health and mental health is critical to well-being in certain contexts, which can make it more challenging for a stable individual to adapt to a specific one when people are in a better state of mind, they are better able to co-ordinate with their surroundings.

The definition of mental wellbeing can be described as a ton by knowing one's personal protection as well as well as the ties to the family. People are expected to extend their home and family position by taking on an important role in the family. This is important because it improves self-esteem and promotes emotional wellbeing in children. and whether they handled him/her well when he/she was young or badly when he/she was younger, his/her parents' care giving position is important for her/his/his/his siblings' and other family members may play a part in her/his/his present shyness, boldness, fear, and anxiety, they have been raised, and there was significant help for him/her younger, tidiness, insecure, and sicker sibling if their behavior towards him/her had been emulated as a child or they had neglected, the earlier, fearful, and sicker sibling As a consequence, behavioral wellbeing approaches in various societies use different principles. Overall, it's interpreted as feelings of becoming happier, well balanced, as a feeling of being healthy and contented, or stronger trust in stable circumstances. Over the course of a lifetime, in order to acquire self awareness, workable life ambitions, handle an environment, and constantly preserve personal character, and learn and development, one must not skip chances to become accustomed to certain causes.

1.4.1 Characteristics of Mentally Healthy Person

claim a person who is psychologically stable is often leading a balanced, healthy existence has the following characteristics. To put it another way, the individual has a feeling of satisfaction."

- a great interest in making a good life and an aptitude for enjoying oneself

- the desire to recover from difficult situations or recover quickly from adversity
- a unified feeling of task and honesty in both job and interpersonal relationships
- an eagerness to learn mindset to embrace modern technology and an adaptable disposition
- a harmony of labor and leisure, on one hand, and relaxation on the other hand
- Able to both create and sustain trusting and enjoyable personal relationships a person with self-esteem and trust in their ability

1.4.2 Diabetes and Mental Health

A diagnosis of diabetes may have a significant impact on one's life. Type 1 or type 2 diabetes, either way, will affect your relationships and your general well-being. Think of it this: When you set a daily schedule, it is vital to get into the practice of maintaining your emotional well-being. When you are conscious of the symptoms, effective diabetes treatment is needed. Much as for blood glucose levels, it is important to monitor your emotional and psychological well-being. Taking care of your mind is just as vital as caring for your body. Treatable problems like stress and anxiety don't seem to improve diabetes.

Mental disorders such as depression and anxiety are undertreated among diabetics because of their reduced rates of diagnosis. At least 45% of the cases of psychiatric illness and emotional impairment are never known because a patient has diabetes. Diabetes recovery teams must be mindful of the relation between mind and body, and take into account the body's overall well-being as well. It may be done in one of two ways: one is to scan for mental health issues through routine checkups, or the other is by doing regular checkups for mental health problems. Diabetes is considered to be a very frequent source of mental health problems for those who don't pursue medical assistance. The individuals who suffer from too-high or too-low blood sugar levels are often asymptomatic. People with diabetes may often experience discrimination and may be hesitant to express their feelings of distress in public environments. Diabetes is said to be caused by excessive sugar in the blood. All the brain does utilize, like thought, judgment, feeling, and behavioral processes, is made from glucose. If there is so much glucose running into our veins, our brain would often suffer. There are many aspects that diabetes will affect a person's general mental health:

- Depression - People with diabetes have a better chance of experiencing depression is one of them getting it. Because of these results, scientists' hypotheses say that a potential connection between stress and the brain activity fluctuations of people with respect to diabetes and their bloodstreams is still unknown, they conclude that something could be linked. Additional consequences of improperly regulated diabetes may involve the development of signs that seem to be close to depression.
- Dementia - With a growing abundance of studies being conducted, further and accumulating data to confirm this, it, the likelihood of diabetes triggering dementia is higher and well-established. The argument is that chronic tension built up by elevated amounts of glucose on the liver, in this case, may have detrimental effects on the health of the brain. Although it's known that diabetes has a strong links to cardiovascular disease, other researchers have advanced the hypothesis that the diabetes constricts blood arteries which may contribute to the production of hypertension, which induces decreased blood pressure and eventually causes brain injury over time.
- Delirium - Diabetes is often confused with delirium and it is often not properly regulated. Symptoms of profound uncertainty and bizarre enough to warrant an imminent alteration of behavior are impossible to comprehend and correlated with an increased likelihood of long-term neurological decline and death. It is a matter of great concern because delirium sometimes goes undetected, and that there is a short window to cure it within which period of life.

1.5 Concept of Marital Adjustment

Families have been around for hundreds of thousands of years, but the definition has evolved through space and time. Marriage refers to only to a man and a woman, and spouse refers to an individual of the opposite sex who is someone's husband or wife. A relationship is made up of more than just two people. Contentment is a state of happiness that comes from full participation and contribution. When you're young, you find big problems. The older you get, the smaller your problems seem to be. Adjusting one's marital status is an aspect of social health. An upset marital relationship has a negative impact on physical and mental health, and also the life quality of life. A lot of weeks, months, years, and days are often spent in one day. While this phase is going on, the couple comes into close contact, showing everything they've got. When things get big, they matter a lot; when they're small, they don't matter at all Even over small disagreements there is no great remedy. It doesn't matter how anyone can be unintelligent, angry, lazy, short, pompous, and spiteful as long as long as they're married. Errors and failings are apparent in marriage.

Marriage is more of a complex thing today due to the shifts in society. There are various reasons for people to get married. Adjusting to change throughout life, yet in the early years of marriage, you have to pay special attention to it Understanding your spouse is an ongoing process; understanding the trait they may or may have developed over time is possible regardless of your knowledge of them prior to or at the time of the marriage. Since maturity necessitates the ability to grow with your spouse, marital adjustment requires a level of maturity that accepts growth and development. The death of a marriage would occur if this potential was not harnessed. According to an American-Filipino psychologist, the death of a relationship is an excruciatingly drawn-out process, not an instant process of decay. Undetected cancer that kills and silently it's like a silent killer. In addition to sex, security, comfort, economic partnership, protection, escape from loneliness, and children, there are a few more things that can constitute the primary motivations for marriage. Some psycho there pathologists discuss the topic of homogeny. Those people unconsciously prefer those who gratify their needs to falling in love.

A significant factor that can lead to marital tensions and concerns is the role transition between couples' values, attitudes, and beliefs when they first move in together. Happily married spouses have the following beliefs about happiness and expectations. Mutual understanding and communication are essential to making adjustments in a relationship. Studies indicate an outstanding marriage rate for those who interacted well with each other. People who are better communicators have a greater capacity for self-adjustment Couples, who communicated more often, had better problem solving skills. Caring is vital to a healthy relationship. Awareness of the feelings needs, and expectations of those who are cared for are critical to being loved. There are two important components of marriage according to Ramcharan (2008): In religious language, the word 'Bodily' often refers to various wishes related to desires such as for health, salvation, body, safety, etc (love, respect, adore etc.). As you approach the end of life, the late elements will come to the fore (e.g. love, respect, affection, or adoration) Marriage is the most important of all human relationships and should be approached only after careful deliberation. If we wish to have a mutually beneficial relationship, marriage is a process of adjustment for both husband and wife. It's not only the size of the bowl but the depth that counts.

A commitment between two people, who will live with each other in a close relationship for an extended period of time. Each of these people has his/her own unique past and present circumstances. Different families although they may be part of the same social network. All of us have developed certain attitudes and skills in reaction to the events of our lives. The former envisages marriage with ideas of what it is and what they think each other should give, while the latter measures what they will get from it. Wife and husband: It's a two-way street game. In marital adjustment, love, friendship, and sexual necessity are strongly linked One must enter into a union with cooperation, because success in marriage is predicated on "Give and Take." A happy marriage does not come about by chance. It must be cultivated with constant cooperation.

The standard of sexual intercourse is the union between a man and a woman. The institution of marriage is founded on cultural, legal, and religious foundations. While spouses help one another social, physiological, emotional, and security needs are met by each marriage, each couple fulfills their own needs as well. It's the latest controversy about the relative merits of the individual families that's riveting the conversation at the moment. Importance of people's daily lives caused the passage of the UN resolution designating 1994 as the International Year of the Family, thereby contributing to the recognition of family life as a fundamental human right. The number of variables is simply too great to consider at this time. Modifications in your marital status are a part of adjusting to married life. Matrimonial estate, where there is a general sense of happiness and contentment in both spouses. The key to a successful marriage is in one way or another being happy. Mostly people go into long-term relationships because they want to find a lifelong partner. A few expectations are within the realm of possibility and many are totally unreasonable. Marital satisfaction is defined as “a feeling that spouses experience of contentment and delight in their marriage” Adjusting to a marriage is a good thing, but must include growth and development as well as demanding of them. Death is a necessary part of growth if the relationship is not enjoyed. Adjustment to the term used to describe how people fare after getting married. People going through marital life encounter many difficulties such as mate-relationship problems, having to adjust to spouse, parenting issues, adjusting to life in-laws fulfill this need? Where do we have in common? What can you enjoy together? Identical values? What role do you want to play? It is the most critical moment in a person's life. One often needs to make several transformations in order to reach the same destination: new relationships, new roles, and new transitions in order to succeed in marriage. In Hinduism, a daughter-in-in-law is the same as that of a girl; additionally, it's a brother's role. Communion has two goals in mind: first, they hope to understand one another's roles, feelings, commitments, and burdens; and then they want to come to an agreement on how to serve and take care of each other. Stable relationships with men and women are the most important aspect of marriage. Sexuality and creating new generations are among the central purposes of marriage.

1.5.1 Variable Effective les of Marital Adjustment

Psychologists have given different variables as per their different opinions.

(1) R.F.WINCH (1963):

- Sex relations • House hold qualities • Philosophy of life and rearing children • Social activities • Mutual friends • Spending family incomes

(2) LANDICE:

- Religion • Social life • Mutual friends • In laws • Money

(3) TEVARAJ:

- Companionship • Recreation • Parenting • Rearing children • Sexual satisfaction

(4) SIMON:

Training and disciplining of children • Religion • In-laws relationship • Financial matters • Sexual relationship • Communication • Mutual trust • Companionship • Social Activities and recreation

1.5.2 Importance of Marital Adjustment

A successful and happy marriage is everything for men and women to aspire to. The change in marital relationships is extremely vital for married persons. Marriage is the ability to provide a lasting intimate and lawful bond with another individual which is a person's essential need as an adult. People have three primary requirements for marriage: passion, pleasure, and the kids' basic need for physical proximity. At the root, a union, you are trying to get your wife pleasure, and that's what you want to do. Some dreams are true, and some are fraudulent wishes. Don't be in a rush in pursuing a partnership. In reality, remain in it long enough to see if it evolves with time.

In order to maintain marital harmony, it is necessary to make life changes. such as more rights, resources, greater independence, less restriction on selecting a life partner, a growing availability of and confidentiality of internet services, greater sexual freedom, etc. have rendered it difficult to maintain a conventional value and meaning of marriage and family On a global scale, there is a the movement that doesn't place marriage and/procreation on the important items of existence, it believes only in certain pursuits that aren't associated with survival. Other developments that blur the boundary between humans and families are inseparable from parenting, zygotes, gestational carriers, and how full we humans have become as a result of these are on their own or the side of the machine is moving humanity forward to the goal of knowing the current family ethics. A failing in adjustment in one's interpersonal relationships may result in personal suffering, such as depression, anxiety, tension, and addiction one's physical, economic, and cultural stages influence the individual's marriage patterns now more than they did in the past. Healthy married change is the one factor that passes through to a successful life.

1.5.3 The Impact of Chronic Illness on Marriage

People who are coping with a chronic illness or recovering from one can need person or couple's counseling to cope with all of the emotion and power problems that occur. Despite the overwhelming evidence to the contrary, Rolland claims that men are agonized between feelings of inadequacy as family providers and, more often, knowing that it is okay to be cared for while they are sick. This relates to the ways in which women and men balance each other out because men sometimes, women are more capable of providing treatment to a companion instead of taking care of themselves while they are sick. It is said that men choose to employ a housekeeper instead of taking on housework, while the female spouses, often in the presence of a stable husband, have a strong desire to add to do the bulk of it themselves; housewives, nevertheless, almost all work themselves. Becoming despondent as they believe that they have negatively impacted their husbands and contribute to feelings of remorse and anger in the husbands from doing something they may not have done due to their spouses (Rolland, 1994). Possible reasons include: The genders seem to respond to sickness in completely differently, so some of them may need to be counseled with their partners, while others may choose to only take care of them. In addition to having physical and psychological issues, often sexual difficulties as a result of being sick, certain individuals may no longer meet their partner's needs. May lead to destructive patterns of promiscuity in unhealthy marriages (Rolland, 1994).

It is obvious that it is more difficult for middle-aged and older adults to prosper while their spouses are diagnosed with long-with-illness because they can't get along as well with them, and even partners in long-who-survive-problems leaving unions are far less frequent. Even people of unhealthy partners are greatly impacted by their diseases, reports researchers noticed in a report by Baetsel (1989). This research examined people over the age of 68 who were male on the following observations: These mean ages of the men: Mean age was 68 years and on the participants. This thesis utilized cancer as a vector for sickness since it expresses itself over time and above brief amounts of time. While Baider et. al.,(1989) learned that wives and husbands shared, to be short, the extent of emotional tension was limited, as well, while the husband was sick, he and she only felt it appropriate to increase her blood pressure. In contrast to their non-exposed mates, it was discovered that both partners recorded greater degrees of anxiety and concerns that may be categorized as psychological.

1.6 Concept of Life Satisfaction

"Satisfaction" is the type of feeling a person may get when he or she gets everything she desires, which is to say, she does not want more than she has already. We are talking about something broader here, which is wanting something that already and finding someone wonderful. Well-beings are almost as essential to general human satisfaction. Any people cannot get what they are looking for. The individual would then go through much emotional suffering as a result. You may experience a feeling of happiness if you happen to be in the right position or when something exciting occurs. Some people benefit from nothing, and gain little satisfaction, however a significant percentage of people are unsatisfied.

On the one hand, these are the objective facts and on the other, the feelings we get through fulfilling our objectives. Life satisfaction represents people's overall pleasure, their ability to be free of life's stresses, their engagement in life, and their involvement in it. In layman's terms, it is to be the perception of your own personal capability for being physically healthy. A big variable in the degree to which individuals' desires are fulfilled tells how happy the individual is, and the person's own personal expectations are satisfied. when we are never able to be really satisfied when we are able to maintain and improve our social relationships [in the present times] society has made so much use of modern technologies and knowledge, however, but this is only useful because of how little thought is paid to social ties Aristotle believed that our society has produced an individual, pouty egotistic, self-obsessed, and daydreaming person of each.

"Happy existence" is one of the key indices of economic well-being utilized in the area of happiness economics. It depicts how happy, fulfilled or contented people are with their lives. When people start thinking about their existence as a mix of something that comprises several different elements, they begin to get a broader outlook on their happiness. the extent to which they achieve their aspirations, or their overall life happiness depends on how good they are performing, or whether they are getting by on in their current situation is only a reflection of the amount they have currently doing is a significant component. Generally speaking, the amount of time and effort put into a job has an impact on how happy someone is at work. Researchers can't predetermine the individual elements of social services. Most respondents may respond that they are pleased when they're able to answer "I am content with my life as a whole, and to the degree that it is available," though, surveys cannot assess if individuals are happy with such answers. Life happiness is referred to as the overall sense of well-being, and includes the subject's state of mind, including a personal appraisal of the appreciation.

1.6.1 Mental Fulfillment for Life Satisfaction

People get all the computers so they cannot achieve complete happiness in existence after that. So the philosopher actually claimed that the machinery could not produce pleasure, harmony, joy, but could benefit from the human mind. Satisfaction-in satisfaction, the sorrow of pleasure relies on the mental individual. We have to benefit from what we have to get pleasure and fulfillment. For pleasure and fulfillment, we can stop contrasting ourselves with others. We can't satisfy all desires in our minds. It is not easy since people's minds are made in this direction, often they like opposite. Therefore, it is not necessary to live absolute happiness.

1.6.2 Factors Affecting Life Satisfaction

Life happiness has two distinct components. Both personal and environmental aspects affect the contentment of our well-being.

❖ Personal Factors: Satisfying desires - conflicts and concerns are often created by our needs or impulses. We are unhappy and unhappy about it. The below are the different needs:

❖ Physiological - needs includes food, clothing, dwelling & sex.

❖ Psychological - needs include self-esteem, attitude, social intelligence, mental health, anxiety, frustration, life skills, and emotional stability.

❖ Social -It's additionally necessary to have stable family relationships (good with family, excellent at providing and receiving care, capable of facilitating support, and a high social engagement, among others), as well as positive social skills (fulfilling, productive, positively engaging, and having connections with others)/

❖ Education -In many people's lives, schooling is now has been shown to be a significant in shaping their happiness and well-being. Although education is definitely critical for everyone, each individual develops his or her own approach to learning at a different pace. It erases the human assumptions and cultivates their replacement, so its impact is a person's mindset, intelligence, mentality, and even happiness is what builds things up.

❖ Nature of Job –A great deal of life fulfillment is derived from one's occupation, but the degree of satisfaction with that occupation still matters. The primary goal of any social animal is to be respected and esteemed by its peers, which can be obtained by formal or informal rank, high or low status. Job advancement is vital for men, especially for the well-being of those in the middle and upper middle class. Through this, I mean, being able to provide you with a decent and appropriate work would provide you with an acceptable amount of happiness in life.

❖ Economic Status -the three goals of happiness: Satisfaction with your home and your financial situation, enough to get by, and the ability to create your own lifestyle.

❖ Environmental Factors: Anything that is around us is a part of the environment falls under the definition of the environment. According to recent research, it has been shown to have a significant impact on a variety of personality characteristics, and our general social well-being. This is especially true when the atmosphere is quiet and pleasant. This helps balance life when the environment is calm and serene. Powerful mutual connections with neighbors, working with coworkers, and involvement in social events all give one a sense of mission and pleasure.

- Social Circle/Friendship -To be happy with what one has is, and respect what one has; contentment with friends and with the availability of time to experience them.
- Occupational Facilities -Satisfied living is improved such as advancement, respect, independence, pay, safety at the workplace, employment position, head friendliness, staff relations, accomplishment and working standards.
- Community Environment -comparable to the degree of satisfaction that the residents have with municipal services such as garbage collection, road conditions, such as the weather, public transportation, public confidence, security, and neighborhood life.

1.6.3 Importance of Life Satisfaction

Generally speaking, a person's happiness with life encompasses all that they are interested in their lifetime. The extent and value of occurrences of bad emotions are more likely to deter you from being happy and therefore distract from pleasure, which are necessary ingredients in increasing wellness it's a problem of great significance in today's hectic circumstances. If you don't experience happiness, you cannot lead a quiet and tranquil existence one must become an adept at breaking the cycles of stress, anxiety, fears, and anxieties in their everyday life when this occurs, it can lead him to be unable to go on.

Happiness applies to an individual's well-being, the standard of life, and what one is grateful for. Human life is only ever described by the achievement of enjoying it, for the pure delight of finding happiness, not by the perfect absorption of others. Self-expansion: Without balanced self-growth, both the inner and outer self are maladjusted if you encounter boredom in your life, so your purpose is in life is uncertain. The results of research also shown that what kind of interaction tension people have with their families would have an impact on their overall level of happiness, as well as how they cope with the kind of conflict in their families force them to confront. The standard of successful life is higher, too, for those who cope well with work-family tension.

1.7 Concept of Adjustment

As far as we're concerned, an improvement would still involve the following: appropriate, enhancing, adjusting, harmonizing, changing, or calibrating. The definition of this term can be expanded, modified, controlled, or resettled in certain cases. the words of this define the capacity to maintain touch with his/to integrate various circumstances There is also the implication that an adjustment term emphasizes the individual's own struggles with his/achievements in his/her social and physical environments. As one scholar puts it, variously, the term change has been applied to by psychiatrists, biologists, as well as health care professionals, have talked of.

Biologists use adaptation of the real universe to describe the phenomenon of expansion. Some argue that culture and its expectations are pushing individuals to be different; some claim the ordinary individual is performing fine in their capacity to respond to social expectations. Concepts relating to behavior are opposed because behavioral scientists sometimes disagree on whether their meaning needs to be empirical, detailed, with diverse viewpoints that vary greatly, arguments exist, and aren't coherent. One thing that this theory has struggled to do is to do is to provide a complete description of change. Expanding the limits are partly because the many meanings of the phenomenon and often open up, and partly due to the fact that criteria are vague, but overall the lines of demarcation are not well established.

In the first two senses, the term "adjustment" is to a means to create, to accommodate, alter, or modulate, and to prepare, and change, and in the latter two senses, to accomplish the same task expansion may be thought of as a purposeful and complex act by which an organism attempts to establish equilibrium with its surroundings The route he chooses to get there can range from being the cause of his failure to working perfectly. Some cases can require the adjustment of several times over many months; everybody, on the other hand, is faced with several demands to adapt. For the good of the whole civilization, the human universe to extend and absorb overhanging circumstances, performance is of the utmost importance a potential adjustment means the degree of a person has achieved with regard to the complexities in his existence a program expansionist has little obstacles to contend with in his endeavors. When it comes to getting people aware of his beliefs, the only real obstacle is the opponent's ingenuity.

In this way, a person's attributes and capabilities are the results of the categories of personality, and his or adjustment modes, such that if the latter is extended, the former often are. It is also seen as a gradual readjustment in which the person must take everything in stride, conform to both himself to the world and his wants, or her, and advance accordingly. The word change is relative and adjustable each period the person has to overcome new dilemmas and comes up with new tactics to conquer them. Any time we have to contend with the large issues of our lives, we have to re-look at the forms in which we view, respond, and fully meet the demands on us. We adjust when our existence depends on it, so our existence is dependent on how it is altered. To have a nice life, a man must be responsive to his social atmosphere is as well as personal environment.

1.7.1 Process of Adjustment

The process of adjustment is critically important to psychiatrists, students, and likewise, it is crucial for both. If we want to get a handle on the mechanism, we can look at the growth of a person from infancy to adulthood. During his time of birth, the infant is entirely reliant on others for the items like his nourishment; however, hygiene, protection, and general well-being become more self-sufficient as he develops. A major part of his recognition and sensitivity to the social conditions relies on how he communicates with the surrounding community. Birth is the most complicated time of everything, because until he is in the universe, everything occurs at once. As he becomes older, he will no longer notices as a wide and distinct differences in the finer things, such as seeing new, distinguishing, and processing perceptions, he will become more able to explain the differences he finds. The method of reevaluation will uncover the existence of the below four major characteristics:

(1) Motives - The adjustment of the human being occurs by some sort of reinforcement or assistance.

(2) Thwarting conditions - When the world is filled with block, people see what is required and no obstacle is to it, so the changes are normal and easy to accomplish. However, if the present conditions get in the way of the achievement of our objectives, then the requisite strategies for overcoming such impediments are implemented.

(3) Response - A negative reaction or interpretation, including anxiety or rejection of emotional encounters provides opportunities for various purposes. Which answers have been given to the block? Some of these reactions may be natural, while others may be considered irregular.

(4) Solution - He is therefore able to manage different scenarios and incidents, some of which drive him farther away from those that lead to getting him up to speed. There is no longer a matter of change to be addressed.

1.7.2 Characteristics of a Well-adjusted Person

These are all correlated with improved mental wellbeing and well-being, but none of them can be seen on their face it might be helpful to learn about his own talents and weaknesses. The true expression of human identity is understood by an entity when he recognizes what is strong about him and what is not, and what is missing. Through using his assets and choosing places in certain other areas where he has the advantage, he seeks to extend his selection. And self-respect and consideration towards others. Being unhappy with one's self is almost all a result of poor transition. The person is well conscious of the obligations put on him by having consideration for his own integrity and wants to demonstrate dignity to others. Acceptable suction levels of aspiration He doesn't show appreciation or reverence for his skill in any situation, and has a significant degree of trust in himself. This trait seems to be out of character for him. Nevertheless, he doesn't seem concerned about whether he'll rise to the high level of success and fame or sink to the low level of regret about it.

Unsatisfaction of simple necessities there are all of his vital physical, mental, and personal needs addressed, as well as all of his cultural and group criteria fulfilled. He does not have any personal requirements and does not suffer from loneliness. He looks as though he has his own reputation and self-worth preserved. Without exception, every participant congratulated him when he entered, and displayed a complete lack of any sort of critique or disappointment when he left. He values the good and beneficial qualities of everything, whether it is an entity or an individual, or both. Instead, he searches at different explanations why things may not be the way they want to be. He presents an observation concerning research rather than berating or criticizing it. He respects the individuals he meets and he likes, as well as their commendable attributes. One of the characteristics of students that benefit from extroversion is flexibility in actions. He's not the kind of person who sticks to his beliefs or morals/ he's not the kind of person who abides by her beliefs or her morals He has the potential to respond rapidly and favorably or neutrally to changes in the conditions, having honed his actions to meet the particular needs of the case. There is nothing that ever worries him and gets the better of him, even for unfavorable situations, even though it means standing up to combat it. Because his genes push him to get a handle on everything around him, he is very serious with environmental mastery rather than merely taking place by accident. Seeing items as they actually are rather than as they can seem to be His perception of truth is very modest; he doesn't get carried away by fantasy. And though he has grand designs, he still cautiously plots his approach.

A person who is well-adjusted likes and comfortable with his surroundings. He comfortably blends in his domestic surroundings, as well as in his neighborhood and in his own house and with his relatives. If a student enjoys his schoolmates, his instructors, and he's happy with his everyday schedule, that is what he really needs. Despite all of the challenges, his career entry into a role is enjoyable and thrilling, and engaging to him, and that stays relevant during his time in it. A moderate yet well-rounded worldview such an individual has a sense of purpose so he can use conditions to help him lead, but remains aware of it while using his ideology as a compass. Since he can always succeed against society's constraints, since this theory centers on the needs of community, history, and his own beliefs, he doesn't battle with himself or conflict with his current atmosphere.

1.8 Concept of Death Anxiety

There is proof that death has proved to be a strong throughout history as a profound motivator for dreaming creatively and undertaking thorough and careful philosophic research. It is often argued that three days prior to Ivan Lynch's suicide, Leo Tolstoy, a 19th century Russian author and moral theorist, made a poignant expression of human problems in his own time about facing certain death by writing about the last of the aging Ivan Lynch's dilemmas. An experience of the futile fight against death was incorporated into this story about Lynch's son was about his implicit influence, unnoticeable force in pushing his son into a private black bag, and he too was called 'resolute' death consciousness may be classified as "anxiety," and acts as a mirror by which individuals can observe their lives, search for solutions to avoid, and measure their chances of death (Abdel-Khalek, 2005). The idea of finiteness or finitude is something special to humans, who must strive to survive and conform to the notion of their own in order to better their lives.

1.8.1 Attributes of Death Anxiety

Six symptoms of death anxiety were found: strong emotions, socio-cultural growth, social factors, experiential learning, and education about death, as well as socio-psychological and the cause of one of motivation was cited.

❖ Emotion - A deep rooted and innate part of the individual's psychology connects him or her to annihilation, originating in ancient, hardwiring, and modified during one's lifetime to take into account the most significant threat of her existence (Panksepp, 1998). structure that are connected to subconscious (unconscious) fears are involved in the formation of the creation of permanent (conscious) fears is critical in understanding this underlying neural system including the amygdale and its associated mechanisms that help with unconscious fears to form clear (conscious) memories are connected to the hippocampus. Both fear and anxiety can be triggered by the same stimulus in our respective emotional memory mechanisms in the event of death (In humans, the two emotions are provoked in response to the same threats, which operate in tandem, simultaneously) (LeDoux, 2008). When we recognize the existence of death, anxiety would be more entrenched in our memory, thus generating new death-related anxiety which serves to cement itself further (e.g., Panksepp, 1998). Implicit and explicit emotional memory mechanisms are needed for fear signaling and control, and both of danger is present in all social learning (Ohman, 2000). Research has so far shown that it is only over the course of animal experiments that emotional processes may be de-paired of their interaction (LeDoux, 2008). Of course, people will feel distress in the face of death. For others, it may be more acute because of overt (end of life) or true fear; some will merely be caused by latent (previous experiences of) fears. There is a distinct emotional dimension of our human memory patterns of thinking that prepares us for potential threat and circumstances, as well as a more cognitive facility that forecasts and preps us for future difficulties.

❖ Cognitive-First thesis is a thorough analysis of Kelly (1955) went on to prove that death was incompatible with simple structures and processes, and often means that living beings cannot sustain their frameworks over time. Many, an integrated, holistic learning are available from life's interactions and constantly changing; therefore, those who will have to expand their notions of human limitations find it more difficult to gain greater mental capacities. To the people Mortality is not only becomes less of a problem in people's worldviews as it is identified as being woven into the fabric of the way of life in which they live their whole lives (Kelly, 1955). a cognitive framework that underlies in the fact that people have varying needs for order and structure, as well as for ambiguous information and for making sense of complexity, may affect a person's understanding of danger and their anxiety level (Jost et. al., 2007). significant anxiety cognitive facets of death involve getting a positive or negative perception of one's own potential mortality, presumed power, anticipation, and obligation for the other's death, and severity of death, and desire for an outcome conceptions about death include assumptions about the afterlife, recollections of departed loved ones, impressions of the dead, and perceptions of no longer being among the dead people of the universe.

❖ When people with general fear worry of their own the dying, they may believe that their emotions would either disappear or change and their loved ones' ingloriousness. When they're anticipating the demise of a loved one, they expect the thoughts of the process to be distressing and their thoughts about the self to be out of being dead. But, while they have death-related concerns, such as those about the annihilation of identity or conscious death after death, their cognition is dynamic. Research demonstrates that an individual's attitudes about death are more reliably determines his or describes his or her apprehension of multidimensional death than influences such as age, position, ethnicity, socioeconomic status, or role in society. Death fear is generated by the thought of not possessing the potential to predict and foresee the future. Death is generally seems to be more prevalent because of this, resulting in increased levels of death salience.

❖ Experiential-humans go through life unbothered by death because they are not terribly afraid of it; this serves an adaptive purpose of limiting paralyzing fear and terror which helps to allow people to get through of extended mindset The solution one takes to thinking about death-threatening thoughts includes conscious protections like diversion, which only helps regulate conscious distress, but does little to cope with the other kinds of terror, which is done in other venues, such as hallucinations. In other words, it consists of a capacity to establish limits on one's behavior, including self-control and the ability to hold off fear of death, to protect themselves from the threats of anxiety and stress, and, and maintain an assertive stance against the anxieties which result from interfering with or upsetting their life. Studies suggest that worrying about the fear of death is related to the build-up of depression and a longer duration and lessened sleep in individuals who hold these feelings over prolonged periods of time. Although a central human fear of becoming devalued by society's expectations may play a role in shaping cultural-derived self-esteem, it is fundamentally protective in nature and helps to deter one from becoming harmed by others in the community. It has been shown that having a high sense of belongingness has been found to be related to decreased death anxiety.

❖ Developmental - the expression of death fear changes according to the age of the infant or teenager Childhood is described as a period of identity expansion and consolidation during which some life events a child must encounter and work through to overcome, according to experts in the field of developmental psychology. the evidence derived from Erikson's research on generatively tasks in mid-life projected a generative understanding of mortality (trade) The current concept of death awareness resulting in crisis, and immobility (early or late), as opposed to the more conceptual "stagnation" or "integrity" concept," had emerged in later. People in their 40s and up focus on how their life was at a time where they were more caring and loyal to the world. They see the world as they did when they were going through their younger adulthood when the stage of having to serve someone greater than themselves. Death anxiety has been supported by developmental theory, meaning, in which it was found that there is a negative correlation between expectations of existence, intention, and middle-oriented individuals' levels of well-age, according to the research on Erikson has conducted on young and old adults. Late in the life people have been shown to struggle from not having been comforted and nurtured early in their life, and hear from worries attributable to abandonment and deaths later on. Weariness grows as people give up their traditional forms of protection, and individual's progress further and develop beyond their cultural and familial boundaries.

❖ Socio cultural Shaping-According to cultural differences, everyone's beliefs on mortality, whether or not, there are many experiential, perceptual, and even emotional facets to death. Culture is the most important to aid in shielding people from the experience of information and the fear of death. The initiatives placed in place to encourage preservation of the distinctiveness and to provide existing cultural safeguards are strongly related to theological and studied interpretations as well as the unknown ones, and many of which are drawn from hypotheses about the culture's roots. Dread in people's minds plays a central role in assisting with their fear of mortality. In particular, researchers have noted the influence of individual meaning orientations and attitudes on people's anxiety about death serves to enhance or diminish terror control.

- Source of Motivation - anxiety about death plays a part in helping people to live thus, death fear is present at birth and mostly because it is viewed as a clear fact of life is difficult to grasp, and thus it emerges as a goal to acquire in the creative domain. It becomes more evident as the individual grows older and takes on more and more items. Evidence is converging to support the hypothesis that multiple causes are linked to the need to the need to stay alive for different individuals and well being when one's own identity, motives, and defensive strategies are attributed to varying behavioral patterns in a number of persons.

1.8.2 Diabetes and Death Drive

Death provokes unreasonable responses in certain people; of which he understands little but which terrifies him, there is no means of accounting for it. Therefore, everybody is scared of dying. Death is a threat which can cause the loss of the actor's sense of well-being which forces the actor to feel unfulfilled or unknown. For instance, those experiencing a disease where there is a clear prognosis in which there being little possibility of cure or healing, certain people can forgo medical care to seek the easier life-expanding propensity of driving away in order to enjoy their final days; and, as this occurs, problems may occur from the anatomy, such as the patient death. A debilitating condition instigates or causes incidents arise. When the trouble is here, it's his is to struggle, because it's to his benefit to strike. Plus, the pain always comes with the disorder. He always needs to lose his life when his mates are battling, and others perish because of his loved it. As the lures the reflection calms Peep, as well as does medicine or a chronic patient, Peep is a kind of a mental protective net for him, shows he feels relief with respect to his visual marks of nonverbal contact of their emotional discomfort and metaphysical depths related to the disease and being unneeded anxiety for him.

1.9 References

Aalto, A. M, Uutela, A, & Aro, A. R. (1997). Health related quality of life among insulin-dependent diabetics: disease-related and psychosocial correlates. *Patient Educ Couns,* 30, 215-225.

Abdel-Khalek, A. M. (2005). Death anxiety in clinical and non-clinical groups. *Death Studies,* 29, 251–259.

American Diabetes Association (2007). Standards of medical care in diabetes-2007 [Position Statement]. *Diabetes Care,* 30:4-41.

Belir, S., Erfani, N., & SafaeeRad, I. (2016). Investigate the relationship between cognitive distortions and quality of life among postmenopausal women, infertility, underwent hysterectomy,

Belir, S., Erfani, N., & SafaeeRad, I. (2016). Investigate the relationship between cognitive distortions and quality of life among postmenopausal women, infertility, underwent hysterectomy,

Boulton, A. J, Vinik, A. I, Arezzo, J. C, Bril, V., Feldman, E. L, Freeman, R., Malik, R. A, Maser, R. E, Sosenko, J. M, Ziegler, D. (2005). Diabetic neuropathies: a statement by the American Diabetes Association. *Diabetes Care,* 28:956-962.

Boulton, A. J, Vinik, A. I, Arezzo, J. C, Bril, V., Feldman, E. L, Freeman, R., Malik, R. A, Maser, R. E, Sosenko, J. M, Ziegler, D. (2005). Diabetic neuropathies: a statement by the American Diabetes Association. *Diabetes Care,* 28:956-962.

Gkaliagkousi E., Ashish S., Alberto F. (2007) Pharmacological and no pharmacological treatment of endothelial dysfunction: relevance to diabetes. *The British Journal of Diabetes and Vascular Disease,* 7:5-10.

Glasgow, R. E., Fisher, E. B., Anderson, B. J., Lagreca, A., Marrero, D., Johnson S. B., Rubin R. R., & Cox D. J. (1999). Behavioral science and diabetes: contributions and opportunities. *Diabetes Care,* 22:832-843.

Haus, J. M., Solomon, T. P. J., Marchetti C. M., Edmison J. M., Gonzalez F., & Kirwan J. P. (2010). Free fatty acid induced hepatic insulin resistance is attenuated following lifestyle intervention in obese individuals with impaired glucose tolerance. *Journal of clinical endocrinology and metabolism,* 95 (suppl 1):323-327.

Jost, J. T., Napier, J. L., Thorisdottir, H., Gosling, S. D., Palfai, T. P., & Ostafin, B. (2007). Are needs to manage uncertainty and threat associated with political conservatism or ideological extremity? *Personality and Social Psychology Bulletin,* 33, 989–1007.

Karlon, H. J., Mohsen, B., and Cherpitel J. C. (2001). Alcohol, Tobacco, and Drug Use and the Onset ofType 2 Diabetes among Inner-city Minority Patients, *JABFP*, 14(6)430-436.

Kelly, G. A. (1955). *The psychology of personal constructs* (Vol. 1). New York: Norton. *23, 10*89–1207.

Laakso M. (1999). Hyperglycemia and cardiovascular disease in Type 2 diabetes. *Diabetes*. 48:937-942.

LeDoux, J. (2008). Remembrance of emotions past. In K. Fischer & M. H. Immordino-Yang (Eds.), *The Jossey-Bass reader on the brain and learning* (151–179). San Francisco:Jossey-Bass.

Ohman, A. (2000). Fear and anxiety: Evolutionary, cognitive, and clinical perspectives. In M. Lewis & J. M. Havilland-Jones (Eds.), *Handbook of emotions* (573–593). New York: Guilford.

Panksepp, J. (1998). *Affective neuroscience: The foundations of human and animal emotions.* New York: Oxford University Press

Peyrot M., & Rubin R. R. (1999). Persistence of depression in diabetic adults. *Diabetes Car,*22:448-452.

Ramcharan, D. (2008). *Is late marriage advisable? - Ask or Answer Agony Aunt Question.* 24:458-472.

Richard R. R. (2000) Diabetes and Quality of Life, *Diabetes Spectrum,* 13:21.

Rolland, J. S. (1994). In sickness and in health: the impact of chronic illness on couple's relationships. *Journal of Marital and Family Therapy*, 20(4), 327-347.

Tuomilehto, J., Lindstormj, M., &Erikssonj, F. (2001). For the Finnish diabetes study group: Prevention of type 2 diabetes mellitus by changes in life-style among subjects with impaired glucose tolerance. *NEJM,* 344:1343-1350.

Ventura, A. D., Nefs, G., Browne, J. L., Friis, A. M., Power, F., & Speight, J. (2019). Is self-compassion related to behavioral, clinical and emotional outcomes in adults with diabetes? Results from the second diabetes MILES—Australia (MILES-2) study. *Mindfulness*, 10(7), 1222–1231.

World Health Organization (1999). *Consultation Group: Definition, diagnosis and classification of diabetes mellitus and its complications, 2nd ed. Part 1: Diagnosis and classification of diabetes mellitus* WHO/NCD/NCS/99. Geneva: World Health Organization.

World Health Organization. (1952). Constitution of the World Health Organization. In *World Health Organization: Handbook of Basic Documents.* 5th ed. Geneva, Palais des Nations, 3-20.

CHAPTER – 2

REVIEWS OF LITERATURE

LIST OF CONTENTS

Chapter-2

2 Review of Literature

Two terms are enough to describe the term “the analysis of literature”: “review” and “review of literature.” The word "literature" in research methodology requires a theoretical, realistic, and study-based expertise. This chapter deals with the literature relevant to the issue for a deeper explanation, and explanation of the findings is included in this section. A researcher discovers some of the literature that could be very helpful to this investigation the researcher performed an exhaustive literature review to elicit useful knowledge from the patient. The literature applicable to this project has been prepared and located in the following.

1. Research related to Diabetes and Quality of Life
2. Research related to Diabetes and Mental Health
3. Research related to Diabetes and Marital Adjustment
4. Research related to Diabetes and Life Satisfaction
5. Research related to Diabetes and Adjustment
6. Research related to Diabetes and Death Anxiety

2.1 Research related to Diabetes and Quality of Life

Additionally, quality of health is strongly causes that are specifically linked to the short-term and long-term treatment of diabetes include obesity and obesity-related risks, insulin and insulin based diabetes. Although micro vascular and macro vascular disease problems are very common in the life of a patient with this disorder, they only get more influential when the more the time of illness is involved. It is popular knowledge that diabetes brings in a steep implications for the overall quality of life. Many patients who suffer from chronic illness are concerned about their quality of life while making choices about care, and therefore, a quality of life evaluation can be an essential. patients assert that there is strong proof that mental health issues such as stress are correlated with the frequency of hospitalization and mortality of diabetics agree (Richard and Rubin, 2000).

Quality of life problems are critical because they have a significant long-term effect on the ability to keep people safe and guarantee that their optimal wellbeing for a lifetime. Quality of life is now enjoying a place at the table with other results that affect wellbeing, and well-being in its own right is seen as a means to understanding it. It is increasingly necessary to keep an eye on the condition of people with Diabetes in India because it's on the rise, so attention must be paid to their quality of life. There are various treatment problems with diabetes that concern diabetics, such as unstable insulin levels and exercise intolerance. When schooling and resources are mixed, more prosperity opens up more doors, aging individuals tend to do more badly and have less benefits of well-being; however this might not necessarily be the case (Eljedi et.al, 2006).Diminished health conditions have a small effect on the short- but even in the less on short term Quality of life (QOL) is thought to affect mental, physical, and potential wellbeing, as well as issues such as social anxiety and low self-esteem (Fayers and Machin, 2007). It is also important that many who have not yet obtained a diagnosis have little or no apprehension of coping with diabetes, as that will the continuing suffering and discomfort of others who are actually coping with diabetes-associated diseases.

According to the research by Akinci et .al.,(2008) people who were using insulin have a higher standard of life than those who were using oral hypoglycemic agents in the other side, however, there are several clinical trials showing the state that indicate that patients that use only oral antidiabetic prescriptions do not find much of a change, this lifestyle (among those that have type 2 diabetes). Although the established advantages of early provision, this, initiation is always postponed. Additionally, there are many other variables that impact the patient's quality of life, including conditions that patients have and features that are distinct to each personQuality in life expectancy (Chaveepojnkamjorn et. al., 2008). Many people who are diabetic experience a reduced quality of life and mood disturbances. Thus, health providers should be mindful that individuals with an elevated likelihood of contracting diabetes have higher health issues, and lowered quality of life (Grandy, 2008). Improper anent type 2 diabetes compromises the overall wellness and causes certain complications, including increased illness and lower life expectancy (Mittal et. al., 2010).

There is an equivocal relationship between the administration of medication and the quality of life among diabetics. as has been said that people who used medicine to treat their diabetes faced greater quality of life-of-related problems than those who merely regulated their blood sugar with diet and exercise was prevalent Patients who were less satisfied with the use of the current medicine they were given, as well as being far as being able to decrease their burden of disease, saw much more improvement with insulin therapy In contrast to others who didn't use insulin, male patients have higher quality of life and women on insulin treatment, as well as well as those patients who did not get no other treatment. This was uncovered in a research in Oman which concluded that too much insulin had a similar effect on those suffering from type I diabetes as well as it did those who were diabetics. Patient treatment enhances the individual's capacity to monitor diabetes and the handling of the disease. There was shown to be an increase in problem solving capacity through information, in type 2 diabetes where the schooling of two of type 2 individuals was improved (Al-Maskar et.al., 2011). Any personal variables are correlated with better fitness, such as food, exercise, are linked to an extension of lifespan in people with diabetes. Both food and exercise have been found to increase glycosylated hemoglobin levels, which suggest positive regulation of blood glucose levels in people with diabetes, as well as other well as overall health.

Consequently, efficient self-man agencies (or self-management) are a key in the day-to-to-day sustenance of those who have diabetes. This estimate has been stated to be correct, and it has been suggested that at least 95% of diabetes is a form of self-treatment (Heinrich, 2011). Researchers found that Insulin Therapy through Pills didn't show signs of improving the overall health of diabetics' and may also have been the opposite: Possible drawbacks of insulin therapy, along with issues linked to improved blood sugar regulation, seemed to be higher than previously reported issues with reduced. Because in the general difficulty of controlling blood sugar, having a higher standard of life has not been shown to be related to a more consistent and healthier lifestyle, better blood sugar regulation, or, if pursued, has not really been shown. Some research showed that good glucose regulation was linked to overall wellbeing, with well-being, and complications were found to be the most important for patients' quality of life (Depablos et.al., 2014). Most of the research on diabetes and lifestyle and standard of life and health services in developing countries have been done in areas with proximity to facilities.

Diabetes is more prevalent in developing nations, negatively affecting the standard of life of the patients there. Unfortunately, surveys that analyze the quality of life of diabetics in impoverished countries are ignored in favour of studies undertaken in industrialized countries because, on the one side, diabetics in these countries have a comparatively higher standard of living, yet, on the other, they have a slightly poorer quality of life (Jain et al., 2014). Research find that the disparities in quality of life between diabetics and stable people to be negligible. The strain of depression in those with higher rates of mortality and a while having diabetes is liable for an elevated level of diabetic complications, as well as for declining overall quality of life (Badescu et. al., 2016). This hypothesis was drawn by Fatma Ibrahim et. al., (2016), which suggests that there is a strong connection between 2 diabetes mellitus and lowered quality of life. Extent of harm that is proven through tests that demonstrate how the amount of problems those patients have with diabetes gradually rises and how it affects quality of life (Gebremedhin et. al., 2019). studies but a study in this includes type 2 diabetes adults who are 18 and over, but with a detrimental effects across all three realms of quality of life: physical, social, and environmental for those over age of adult age and on type two patients (Thapa, et.al., 2019).

Girma, like all, (2020) discovered ageing and becoming stigmatized by the media, depression, believing like one's standard of life was compromised, and becoming self-employed have both have a detrimental influence on physical health; while on the other side, getting aged, showing the signs and effects of diabetes, or an extended period of time that people consider when one is unemployed have a beneficial impact on quality of life.

2.2 Research related to Diabetes and Mental Health

Both healthy and unhealthy individuals are at risk of poor mental illness, but those with poor mental wellbeing might be are often more likely to experience complications due to their condition. Researchers also shown that depression is widespread in both in people with type 1 and type 2 diabetes (Lustman, Griffith, & Clouse, 1996). Studies also showed a significant association between diabetes-related neuropathy and depression and in patients that patients with diabetes are six times more likely to develop depressive disorders than those without it. constant weight shift has been correlated with Bid DM type 2-DM depressed symptoms and change in weight has been reported in adults; additionally, studies from the Multiethnic Community, and another report, have indicated that irregular weight gain or loss may also have this connection with type 2 (Golden et al., 2008). Diabetic patients are at risk of depression regardless of all three issues: depression and anxiety getting worse due to the illness, lack of ability to manage the blood sugar, job being worsened due to diabetes, and because of problems arising, and interpersonal issues with their medical management create. Disturbance from diet patterns and phobias including apprehension of diabetes, combined with neurological and emotional problems leading to adjustments such as feeling nervous and unsettled

Until now, most depression treatments have relied on the utilization of a practitioner or a person qualified to administer mental wellbeing care (nurse practitioner) working in tandem. Those may also represent various approaches that use common treatments for people with diabetes that focus on conflict resolution, interpersonal counselling, problem solving, and psychodynamic treatments (Van der Feltz-Cornelis et al., 2010). Meredith, et al. conducted a long-term study in the long term on the connection between depression and type-2 diabetes to clarify the former's relationship with various aspects of the latter. Patients who have a history of previous diagnosis of depression, as well as those who were shown to have encountered poor beneficial impact in the latest studies, displayed a greater likelihood of experiencing potential depression. Diabetes was shown to be linked to the progression of severe depression in subjects who had a mild meditation practice. In studies which investigated whether there is a link between high levels of anxiety and stress in the two separate diseases, Bener, et al. (2011) discovered that there was, in effect, a reduction in both of the DM population subjected to high levels of depression. As it came to the outcomes, almost all the diabetic subjects (33.6 percent) and just 3.9 percent with the non-diabetic subjects of a certain age had moderate-to-to-severe depression (30.9%), as well as almost all the same with any of the other aged subjects (33.6%) were shown to be stressed and anxious. An analysis of the sample uncovered a few linkages, between the variables, demonstrating that, as well as having a strong evidence, which suggested, systolic blood pressure, obesity length, and diabetes duration are predictive of elevated scores in clinical depression among diabetics. It is obesity and smoking that transform systolic blood pressure into systolic pressure into higher blood pressure, as well as elevated tension that account for anxiety and depression among others with regard to these individuals' overall mortality rates among diabetic people.

Everyone with diabetes has to keep their blood sugar levels stable – so psychological approaches are just and important as essential and effective as medical ones in treating the condition. The Anxiety Disorders Association of Unknown of Maryland often claims that anxiety disorders arise, at least partially, are the product of other mood disorders, such as depression. An increased mood and behavioral problems in patients with type 2 diabetes was documented in the previous study that was uncovered in another research study, that stated an increased number of mental health disorders and thoughts of ending one's life among people with type 2 diabetics and potential mental stress that was observed (Cerettaet.al., 2012). Moreover, major disparities were found between the genders so that females had higher depression and anxiety levels, as well as the prevalence of diabetes. In persons with diabetes, the probability of both of being diagnosed with anxiety and depression is double that seen in the general population (Roy and Lloyd, 2012).

Diabetes and related eating habits are twice as prevalent among women with the condition as they are in those without the condition, but in the latter group, they all incidents are more than one and one and a factor and a factor more than that (Goebel-Fabbri, 2013). Boys and men with diabetes are less likely to develop an eating problem than girls and women with diabetes. Disordered eating habits entail excessive eating and limiting the number of calories; those figures range from 31 and 40 percent of women with type 1 diabetes. Nevertheless, no link was found between diabetic complications and stress, or anxiety, and how stressful the diabetic life is for the person in question was in this study Depression and sleep disturbances are often linked to the experience of the severity of diabetes, with possible pre-complications such as kidney disease and vision issues (Rekleitiet.al., 2013). When the analysis was finished, it showed the relevance of the person's personal characteristics to the stress and anxiety rate of diabetic patients. Since the discovery of this relation, there is considerable interest in how the two conditions are related (Ducatet.al., 2014).

People with diabetes are at higher risk of mental health issues, such as depression, than those without the disease, according to previous studies. Glycemic management is an indicator for the likelihood of developing type 2 diabetes, notably for women, diabetics over the age of 40, whose glycemic problems are greater than those of diabetes and those who have trouble knowing what they consume, and for people with chronic mental health concerns, particularly those who are middle-aged. The studies suggest that gender, age, schooling, and diabetes complications raise the risk of the occurrence of anxiety and depression in type 2 diabetes patients (Mikuililin'so, 2014) Some have argued that depression and anxiety cause worse health effects, such as elevated diabetes symptoms, worsening, worse health, higher blood glucose levels, and premature death; however others have disputed this and claim, claiming that it just works in the other direction, causing lower levels.Has been seen to be, as being linked to long-prolonged (Diabetes is a significant as being related to the increased risk of mortality, and long-term mortality has been defined as such (Reisingeret.al., 2015).

Comorbidity observed in the population of people with diabetes in various countries has shown that depression is a commonly co-occurring disease A comprehensive literature review to find for adult type 1 diabetics found that the incidence of depression was 12% Almost three out of every ten people in this demographic were reported to be clinically depressive. The incidence of depression in individuals with diabetes was nearly as high (17.6%) in a literature review and meta-analysis performed in the University of Leicester found (Badescuet, al, 2016). Type 1 diabetes triggers negative emotions including anxiety, embarrassment, remorse, and depression (Friis et al. 2016). aspects of diabetes rather than just don't getting rid of the symptoms (sugar cravings, severe exhaustion, can be included in the concept of major depressive disorders Based on studies by the International Diabetes Foundation, it is reported that one in four people with type 1 diabetes and one in five people with type 2 diabetes will suffer from emotional distress. Anxiety disorders were found in one-third of people with serious mental illnesses and type 2 diabetes, and were associated with increased depressive symptoms and one in five people with type 2 diabetes mellitus(Kreider, 2017) decreased level of function (Bajor et.al., 2018). Various mental health problems have been previously identified as important risk factors associated with poor outcomes in diabetic patients (Smith et.al., 2018). The existence of depressive symptoms reduces cognitive and emotional adjustment to diabetes.

2.3 Research related to Diabetes and Marital Adjustment

Spouses are generally needed to learn to adapt to each other, and work together with one another to increase their capacity for intimacy. Where an individual's happiness in marriage, sexual happiness, and emotional well-being are all associated, you may be included in the expression "an overall feeling of satisfaction with their marriage". Diabetes also influences multiple aspects of sexual health, including impotence, e.g. diabetes-induced urinary tract infection, kidney failure, and vision impairment. The various indices of sexual drive that it targets include are libido, ejaculation, erectile function, and orgasm, as well as sexual appraisal and sexual enjoyment. Dysfunction may be a risk factor for cardiovascular disease, hyperlipidemia, depression, and lower urinary tract symptoms have shown to be similarly to those of all people with these conditions the number of illnesses has been taken into consideration when analyzing the quality of marital relations and recovery in the women in this particular research (Woods, Haberman, & Packard, 1993). Several breast disorders (i.e. to phthisis, mastodynia, fibrocystosis) were diagnosed in the population of working women at this screening, including type 1 diabetes, no mastitis, fibrocystosis, and mastodynia (Woods, Haberman, & Packard, 1993). Female sexual impairment tends to raise the probability of occurring in women for an average eight times of others who are diagnosed with diabetes (Enzlinet,al., 1998).

The age of the women was between 28 and 62 with a median of 41 years and an average of 41 years. Their results showed that all of the women in the study had some moodiness but with relatively strong overall family functioning. to the husband and the diagnosis of sickness required physical disturbance for her (e.g. lying down, frequent observation of symptoms, taking care of other people, etc.), however after dealing with the condition, they concluded that a wife's work and home life was often suffered. More positive outcomes are experienced by people, with their intimate relationships. Both the illness and intimate relationships can influence each other on a bad marital experience and how these elements need to be suppressed (Trief et. al., 2001). Most experiments on sexual issues in type 1 and 2 diabetes patients find the proportion to be 71% and 42% in the respective control groups, with reference to type 1 and type 2 diabetes, although more analysis by Doruk et. al., (2005) discovered that 71% of women with type 1 diabetes and 42% of those with type 2 were impaired, and found the numbers to be the same in both groups. While diabetes is known to influence many aspects of the individual's sex life, such as how one appears, their perception of themselves, their place in society, and relationships with others, it is often important to take into account how it may impact sexual functions.

The other two additional aspects of well-sexual well-being are quality of life and diversity of one's interpersonal relationships. Diabetes is a common problem with regard to overall health because it is involved in sexual dysfunction two times as much as the general public. specific aspects which have distinct roles in overall sexual well-being, while biological processes are significant factors in general, the ways and form of diabetes interacts with psychosocial ones impacts psychological wellness (Giraldi and Kristensen, 2010). Diabetes and rather than gestational diabetes are estimated to be almost double the rate of sexual dysfunction; the amount of this reported in the latter is found to be 26.4%, whereas gestational diabetes has an estimated rate of 49% With respect to Stephenson and Meston (2010), sexual pleasure has an impact on the whole life, but not only on marital satisfaction. Decreased sexual pleasure can also be related to decreased change in the marriage. This may be person characteristics (mood, fulfillment, harmony, love, contentment, on, intimacy, and loyalty) or the marital desires (which can include things like physical attraction, fun, excitement, comfort, excitement, connection, excitement, fulfillment, and contentment). If a woman with diabetes has problems with sexual function, diabetes is a major problem for her sexual well-being.

In contrast, as one views sexuality as a multi-dimensional, the actualized content mention on their sexual desires incorporates more of sexual pleasure and work provides better knowledge on the sexual well- However, whether one is diabetic, it makes the rest of his or her life a difficult because of having diabetes may cause more benign problems such as retinopathy, nephropathy, angina, and myocardial infarction. However, it may contribute to major issues such as nephropathy, micro antipathy, and cerebral infarction. Neuropathy that is induced by diabetes has the ability to create anatomical and functional alterations in the female reproductive system, as well as interfere with sexual reaction.

Women who had more disease demands reported becoming more stressed and less happy with their relationships than women who had less demands. The researchers were able to demonstrate that Dempster et. al., (2011) found that diabetes is directly related to greater likelihood of relationship tension, and marital issues. This book also explored the results showed that married patients who suffer from chronic illnesses and their happiness, however, unfortunately, just quite somewhat, can be relieved by emotional well-being often note minor variations in their degree of stress and other physical pains. abnormalities in women with hypogonatric metabolic conditions and neuropathy is a contributing factor to reduced libido, but women with diabetes who experience it are often particularly prone to have trouble with vascular disease. As a lot of diabetes sufferers (especially women with the disease) are afflicted with sexual problems, as shown by a study conducted on thousands of diabetics (Copelandet,al., 2012). The most important elements of general well-being, if not the major cause, of a healthy sex life (Khodabakhshi-Koolaeeet.al., 2014).

The studies by Pierra et al. performed on women with diabetes Type 2 and their spouses revealed that they were adversely influenced rather than the men with diabetes, finding that married women with diabetes were more anxious than their spouses with diabetes. Diabetes mellitus was correlated with dramatically impacts women's potential for long-expanding a partnership and their marital status, which describes their higher scores on the marital relationship variables than those without it. several reports have found that marital problems in a marriage adversely affects the other facets of it diabetes mellitus 2 research noticed a noteworthy changes in one's rate of happiness, marital satisfaction, and its effect on marital adjustment (Mirghafourvandet,al., 2016).

Recent studies demonstrated that for Type 2 diabetes in women affects women of childbearing age substantially in terms of the sexual function, women of childbearing age were shown to have poorer sexual function than non-diabetic subjects (Afshariet,al., 2017). As is stated in Keyhani et al., (2019) the average levels of both cognitive and affective change were higher than that in non-diabetic people, so that the average cognitive improvement in non-diabetic women was higher than that of the average adjustment in diabetic women. Clinical issues with patients with diabetes endanger these patients from both vascular and nervous system disorders, putting them at a higher risk for psychiatric problems, organic, disease. To be frank, sexual impairment has been neglected in women for several years even though it is commonly seen in them. From my research, there was a study of their presence in women being between 20% and 80% (Rahmanianet.al., 2019).

Several studies have shown a connection improved health outcomes and a greater degree of overall satisfaction of people with their overall quality of life in diabetics who are well-adjusted in their marriage. Also with strong social structures in effect, others may neglect their capacity to cope with the illness and remain in bad health because of the problems that may occur (Triefet,al, 2019). Eminet. al., (2020) recommended understanding the link between sexual life and marital well-being for women with diabetes as well as part of the therapy for this would significantly affect the spouses. Diabetes can become a challenge for patients with sexual disorders due to issues, as it interferes with sexual activity, issues, and ability (Gianattiet.al., 2020) as she described, in her research, noticed that their special disease imposed detrimental consequences on all of their sex life: namely, diabetes had a low quality of life in addition to being difficult to manage and dissatisfaction in marriage Diabetes has risen significantly in Iran and across the globe, proving to be a detrimental influence in many people's lives.

2.4 Research related to Diabetes and Life Satisfaction

Diabetes having a huge effect on patient well-being for providers, especially with regards to the recovery plans for patients that have type-II diabetes, who often miss their drugs or see sub-to-or no adherent doctors (American Diabetes Association, 2010).

As this condition progresses over time and is substantial and permanent improvements in the lifestyle to be created, the patients must cope with specific stress, it is postulated that disability can pose a challenge. the plurality of stressors that patients may experience will have an impact on their quality of life, including lack of social relations, poverty, the analysis of clinical psychology, job frustration, and depersonalization, however, may instead raise the percentage of distress, and decrease the patient' Furthermore, it is Since the findings of numerous studies and study show that different coping responses affect the patient's understanding of their quality of life, it is clear that expectations vary. Since the study suggested that people with diabetes need to engage in longer and more intense psychological functioning in order to deal with the stress that they endure, finding out about how they handle it could be more important for us to learn.

(Chrisma Pretorius1, et, al, 2010).

Thus, the team performed an experiment to investigate the connection between well-being, life satisfaction, the findings of which they compiled in the previously described studies on the mental, social, and physical factors and non-medical dimensions of well-being in the elderly with the participation. This Life Satisfaction Index (LSI) rated it a ten on a scale of one hundred, and then reduced it to a one of ten. the families of and research participants had all been made to feel as well as participants who had been permitted to stay autonomous also gained from the feelings, instrumental and social help to be offered for them The study showed that having low Life Index Score K scores included a connection to low levels of lower satisfaction with the experience of neuropathy and discomfort in the lower back and the knee; having high levels of Community Engagement, interesting relationships, and family/friend involvement and support in a person's involvement with others were associated with higher scores; and having lower K scores were shown to lead to more pain and less satisfactory relationships among the participants. The participants of the diabetes party scored better on the Life Satisfaction Index, regardless of whether or not they were part of whether they had engaged in the test the Life Satisfaction Index.

As compared to those without diabetes, individuals with type-II (who suffer from H.I.I.D.), the patients in Jordan (who have type-II diabetes) reported having "moderate to large" degrees of happiness with their overall existence. Additionally, individuals with diabetes have lower levels of happiness (Holmes-Truscott et al., 2016) Measurement of the degree of a person's life satisfaction and enjoyment are facets of mental wellbeing. A significant thing to keep in mind is that people with diabetes have a propensity to have increased life satisfaction as well as to signal the effectiveness of care, reflecting changes in their wellbeing. The level of life satisfaction shown by people with diabetes increases as it is accurately predicted. It is indicative of excellent fitness, showing that the people receiving treatment have seen success and help, and benefiting from the medications (Rosiek et. al., 2016). A study presented in research suggested that patients with diabetes were more likely to have a desire for self-harm, have lowered quality of life, and suffer from impaired mental wellbeing (Okwaraji et. al., 2017). This research was conducted on 793 diabetics in Jordan and the patients and women, and found no substantial gap in the reported levels of life satisfaction, in spite of differences in overall level of diabetes management.

There are studies out there that focus on three separate areas of sexual well-being, such as function, life satisfaction, and marital satisfaction, but no one that is focused on all three elements. The better clinical results can be traced to better self-management of people's wellbeing, especially with regard to their levels of happiness with their current circumstances, as reported in a lot of scientific literature (2019b). Thus requiring that all type 1 people have access to adequate diabetes therapy, which can provide better well-being for all type 1 patients and patients (2018) more importantly, it is essential to figure out some psychological causes that may help patients with type 1 diabetes lead happier lives after all of the information obtained above. Noteworthy was discovered by the researchers Keyhani et al. (2019) who showed a discrepancy in marital scores for non-diabetic people, allowing marital change in non-diabetic women greater than in contrast to diabetic women. Study showed that the average mean level of life satisfaction of diabetic people was lower than the men who did not have diabetes, according to the data presented by Ozkan and Avcı, (2018). Similarly, the overall scores for diabetics were on the lower end of the spectrum, with moderate life satisfaction. An empirical research paper concluded that people with diabetes were, on average, relatively happy with their lives.

2.5 Research related to Diabetes and Adjustment

It is a common feature in chronic diseases like diabetes that patients must keep up with their care in order to keep their condition under control. progression is to the disease is made up of improvements in healthcare, family structure, intimate relationships, home life, and social networks, as well as well as of transition to the environment. The adjustment to diabetes is determined by several variables unique to the condition, care, and by each patient as a person. It is made up of such variables as the patient's view of their wellbeing and the impact of the disease on it, gender, age, and duration of the condition on different professions. Assessing one's glucose levels and maintaining a specific blood glucose goal rather than simply not going over and below them as much as possible (Pollock et. al., 1990). Understanding the human variables that impact the extent to which one's metabolism will influence one's degree of responsiveness to the disease would allow for the discovery of potential prevention measures to be followed.

White et.al., (1992) published research on female diabetes adaptation. This study showed that the health and psychosocial effects were similar regardless of whether a woman suffered with a chronic disease for a short or long period. On the other hand, the researchers discovered that only a few of the patient's everyday family life was compromised by their disease. From the start, it seemed as though the social roles were uninvolved. At the point of the research, patients were able to convey moderate sadness, low levels of psychiatric problems (miserable emotions of distress, weak self-esteem, or even aggression, did not seem to be troublesome in communities and social relationships. While most chronic conditions need long-term care, stable patient delivery of medication, diabetes often often goes overlooked, with cycles of transition. Both to the detection and management of the disorder ought to be taken into account as well as transition to healthcare, personal relationships, the family, culture, and sex relationships must be included. People with diabetes have the greatest trouble making the metabolic improvements (Willoughby et. al., 2000).

Overall, Adams' research focused on psoriasis victims, with environmental pressures the most, and through his work with these people, he noticed that occupational life and social life both made things greatly improved. When patients who underwent surgery on their larynx were asked to return to work following an initial period of post-surgery recuperation, their psychosocial recovery was shown to be worse than those who did not go back to work. In the case of those who have aged, there are fewer worries because they have already reached life's phases and hence faced the needs of children and other life matters are no longer present to deal with. Results for patients with acute myocardial infarction were shown to be improving, with regard to their emotional well-being, although on the whole, fewer patients may be classified as "well adjusted". The results show that patients with diabetic foot ulcers have a lower capacity to react to life changes than other chronic patients. The Whittemore et. al., (2005) research discovered that age had no major impact on psychological change. As shown in the previous research on diabetic patients, the younger patients demonstrated slightly less adaptation than the older patients. People with diabetes, needing to deal with other conditions as renal failure, neuropathy, and cardiovascular disease, and thereby affecting their quality of life, might have long-has additional long-term impacts on their health.

Lefvre and Levert (2006) focus on six distinct stages that demonstrate the complex and ever-changing essence of the mourning method. Shock, bargaining, denial, remorse, sadness, and change are the fundamental feelings that the early stages of the mourning process include. Type 1 diabetes presents recurring problems in the life of its victims, because patients may be on the transition process their whole life, while they may switch through other phases as their disease progresses. This could render things more difficult and overwhelming for people with each passing day as well as a constant treatment of diabetes continues to contribute to trigger more chaos, sadness, rage, anger, and feelings of resentment. Adverse effects on overall well-being can be experienced due to either to issues created by or the improvements required as patients and their families have to adapt to the treatment. This raises patients' challenges with managing variability in care.

Teens and people in particular appear to have a tough time adapting to shifts in procedures when they're already evolving and are quickly affected by a number of these problems (Goz et.al., 2007).While there being a disparity in the rate of medical regulation, Akça observed that the psychological adjustment to illness was just as prevalent in the patients that she studied. doing routine laboratory testing is crucial for keeping on top of the condition, as well as identifying any potential diabetic problems, and diagnosing it ating it early on handle the health is advantageous for managing disease in the right stage Diabetes must be approached at both angles because of effects it is broad and consequences grow slowly. Transition to it is complicated, and it deals with living in the long term. Short-term and permanent effects are commonly happen, while there are plenty of them, but long-term problems aren't evident immediately. These common trigger factors cause problems in both chronic and acute diabetics and nondiabetic individuals with diabetes lead to a heightened anxiety and social stress because of fear of blood sugar instability and variously ulcers, drugs, disorders, thus preventing psychosocial rehabilitation. Demirtaşe said that the 10-year diagnosis period was extended to the patients at the acceptability standard in order to find diabetic applicants who could survive long enough for. There are five predominant responses to chronic illnesses: shock, denial, frustration, bargaining, despair, hope, optimism, or both, which despair, and then, depending on whether the illness is dealt with as a personal crisis or as well as a major life change, will provide to consumers is a means of coming to terms with something that allows them to establish a feeling of control of their life, as well as there is for victims of any illness. Any amount of time is required to be able to be at last to conform to the fact that the opinions you form about your self are well-supported by evidence.

Researchers around the world have been unable to reach any general agreement on this, although several researchers concur that the recognition and adaptation may be linked to the period of diagnosis. to a great extent, led the country as it's Minister of Foreign Affairs (2010) while older patients have strengthened consistency with a partnership with the diet and with treatment, as well as enhanced capacity to monitor their own feelings, but diag- nosed patients at an early age are more liable to being paranoid and a long-sensitive to the disorder as stated in his work on patients' relationship and health, strengthen and deteriorate in relation to sexual encounters, according to the patient's level of satisfaction in Mauro's research (2010), their well-being and how well they have fared are assessed, or to which they worsen or benefit in terms of his relationship in sexual activities are updated, depend on the patient's level of satisfaction. Another important consideration for individuals is coming to terms with the original diabetes diagnosis and the adjustments required in order being able to cope with such a chronic illness. the lack of preparation to use coping mechanisms may contribute to additional difficulties for those struggling with the problems, and those who still have issues with them would most definitely not be more equipped to tackle the challenges (Bedfordshire Diabetes 2014). The impact of chronic illnesses such as diabetes mellitus on the bio-psycho-social aspects of individual’s health and wellbeing cannot be interpreted solely in terms of disease process, but also relates to difficulties of individuals’ adjustment to their illnesses, and the evolved changes of their lifestyle (Hamdan-Mansour,et,al, 2015). Yanikkerem ,et,al (2016) study showed a positive and significant relationship between sexual function and marital adjustment and a positive correlation between marital adjustment and life satisfaction.

2.6 Research related to Diabetes and Death Anxiety

We pay attention to both short-term and long-term considerations these days with regard to diseases since they are more prevalent than ever before. Additionally, because you can no longer predict when a patient's fear could lead to their demise, we diagnose and manage these conditions correctly by tracking their anxiety levels today. According to recent studies, the diabetic illnesses with the most cases will comprise the bulk of the population by 2020, however because of the amount of risks linked to diabetes they are the most urgent ones. In more recent years, individuals from poorer socioeconomic backgrounds have had to manage numerous financial commitments, families, and other duties. This has significantly affected lifestyle, which has culminated in the increasing levels of Type 2 diabetes around the globe. knowledge of death's eventuality, as a leads people to panic, or to explain their feelings of dread or fear while contemplating the implications (Abdel-Khalek, 2005). An important term used in Freudian psychoanalysis that talks about how humans must become aware of their own limited nature in order to manage the burdens of life (Becker, 1973).

Thus, a crucial for a position in cultural structures is to be provided with a symbolic sense to resolve death and dealing with it in the event while contributing a symbol to the story behind it (Kubler-Ross, 2002). Everyone is afraid of death to a degree. And the terror is no longer deepened when faced by the awareness that there is no way to escape it. Despite the health care technology, longer hospital longevity, longer than average life expectancies, and the almost universal treatment of potentially treatable diseases, mortality remains an ever-present fact for healthcare professionals. There is increasing research in the literature that highlights the essential positions that nurse's play in supporting people and their families to live with mortality and coping with problems relevant to it. Yet before the theoretical and scientific foundations of this literature are discussed, the principles of care and living with death haven't gained as much exposure. It has limited the number of articles to research on death anxiety to that investigates it in scientific investigation work as a broad, an obstacle that may jeopardize anemic healthcare workers' potential to effectively assist a large numbers of those afflicted, as well as their possible capacity to bear up to deal with that particular problem. Since little study has been undertaken to explain this important definition, death anxiety is part of the NANDA outcomes. Despite the critically important theoretical importance of palliative care and science, no precise theoretical description has been proposed. yet should be included in any clinical check-up, in the treatments of cancer patients, in the presence of fear of becoming a long-induced emotional or mental distress, as well as psychiatric, as well as in individuals faced with the challenge of needing urgent help, long-term care, as well as any care of those who are healthy, whether or burdened by stress, cancer patients. Malignor is cited in most Indian studies on mortality and specific variables including caste, gender, form of malignancy, and age appeared at Aligar examined the bulk of the facts in regards Islamic scholarly inquiries on death in the 'counseling'.

Present research shows that gender should not affect death fear, but a fact that individuals with such complex diseases as diabetes, HIV, and cancer, who, in general, suffer higher rates of anxiety. An internet user is not someone who passively gains knowledge on the Internet; rather, it is someone who connects with and, and contributes to, just like an entrepreneur. Many with imminent doom will the end of life encounters are usually higher in terms of death fear, since their health has not changed through the usage of medication, while those who are dealing with severe illness may differ greatly owing to the period that they have until they expire, in their anxiety about it. Our results suggest that men were marginally more prone to experience fear relative to women, to be in some situations, are more frightened than to be nervous, and are closer to death in most cases where they are, in some cases where they did. There are moments where what you desire and what you have are granted appear to be opposites, and this was one of them. A variety of reports indicated that, or research showed, or inferred, that there is no enhanced fear of death in individuals who are dying from any disease. Researchers indicated that there was a higher degree of death fear among people who had illnesses such as depression and anxiety, although others noted that chronic illness caused less of a response (Beydag, 2012).

This association was found by Dogan et al. (2015) who discovered that persons hospitalized with diabetes appeared to have increased amounts of both depression and anxiety. Using normal categorization of death fear of patients with diabetes mellitus, Belir et al observed that there was a major association between cognitive distortion and the patients' level of mortality. There does not seem to be enough neural consistency in the patients for them to be able to face and make decisions; this has caused an increased level of distress to arise. Prevalence of people in the general ranges from 2% to 7% in Isfahan is thought to be approximately equal to the number of people over the age of 30 for both Type I and Type II diabetes, in Type I diabetes, it is considered to be up to 3%. Nervousness. Death fear and the subsequent decline in his/her general success are shown to result in reduced psychological well-being (Poteset.al., 2016). It occurs in people with diabetes mellitus who show a great fear of dying, because of the way the illness takes away their ability to make rational decisions about their health and leaves them in the control of forces outside of their control (Aqajani and Samadifard 2017). Cognitive fusions also have a role in beginning of people's death anxiety.

2.7 References

Adams, T., Glenn, S., & Byatt, K. (2001). The psychosocial adjustment of people with chronic plaque psoriasis. *Clinical Effectiveness in Nursing*, 5, 129–32.

Afshari, P., Yazdizadeh, S., Abedi, P, & Rashidi, H. (2017). The Relation of Diabetes Type 2 with Sexual Function among Reproductive Age Women in Iran, a Case-Control Study. *Advances in Medicine,* 483-492.

Akahashi, M., Araki, A., Watanabe, S., Haga, H., Kimbara, Y., Tamura, Y., Chiba, Y, Mori, S, Ito H, & Shibata H. (2010). Community Participation is Associated with Life Satisfaction in Elderly People with Diabetes Mellitus. Nihon Ronen Igakkai Zasshi. *Japanese Journal of Geriatrics*, 47(2), 140-146.

Akça, Y., Talaz, A., & Çınar S. (2008). Comparison of psychosocial adjustment in people with and without diabetic foot ulseration. *Aust J Adv Nurs,* 25, 87–96.

Akinci, F., Yildirim, A., Gozu, H., Sargin, H., Orbay, E., and Sargin, M.(2008). Assessment of health related quality of life (HRQoL) of patients with type 2 diabetes in *Turkey Diabetes Res. Clin. Pract.* 79(1), 117-23.

Al-Mandhari, A., Al-Zakwani, I., Al-Hasni, A., & Al-Sumri, N. (2011). Assessment of perceived health status in hypertensive and diabetes mellitus patients at primary health centers in Oman. *International Journal of Preventive Medicine, 2*(4), 256-263.

Al-Maskari M.Y., Al-Shookri A, O., Al-Adawi, S.H., & Lin KG. (2011). Assessment of QOL in patients with type 2 diabetes mellitus in Oman. *Saudi medical Journal,* 32(12):1285-90.

American Diabetes Association (2009b). American Diabetes Association; Standards of medical care in diabetes – 2009; *Diabetes Care* 32:S13-S61.

American Diabetes Association (2010). Diagnosis and classification of diabetes mellitus. Diabetes Care. 33: S62–S97.

American Diabetes Association. (2011). Standards of medical care in diabetes. *Diabetes Care*, 34:11-61.

American Diabetes Association. (2019b). Standards of medical care in diabetes—2019 abridged for primary care providers. *Diabetes Care*, 37(1), 11–34.

Aqajani, S., & Samadifard, H. R. (2017). The role of cognitive fusion, locus of control and cognitive avoidance in the prediction of death anxiety in the elderly. *Journal of Health and Care*, 19(1): 62-74.

Ayman, M. Hamdan-Mansour & Dina N. Al. Nawafah Salah I. Hanouneh Hasan D. & Al Omari. (2015). Psychosocial correlates of life satisfaction among patients diagnosed with type-II diabetes mellitus. *International Journal of Diabetes in Developing Countries,* 51 (3):297-334.

Badescu, S. V. C. Tataru, L. & Kobylinska, Te (2016). Association between Diabetes mellitus and Depression," *Journal of Medicine and Life*, vol. 9, no. 2, 120–125.

Bajor, L. A., Gunzler, D., &Einstadter, D. (2015). Associations between comorbid anxiety, diabetes control, and overall medical burden in patients with serious mental illness and diabetes. *Int J Psychiatry Med,* 49:309–20.

Balder, L., Perez, T., & De-Nour, A. K. (1989). Gender and adjustment to chronic disease: a study of couples with colon cancer. *General Hospital Psychiatry*, 11, 1-8.

Bedfordshire Diabetes.org.uk (2014). Diabetes Guidelines, http://www.bedfordshirediabetes.org.uk/guidelines/psychological-issues.html.

Bener, A., Al-Hamaq, A. O. A. A., &Dafeeah, E. E. (2011). High prevalence of depression, anxiety and stress symptoms among diabetes mellitus patients. *The Open Psychiatry Journal*, 5, 5-12.

Beydag, K. D. (2012). Factors affecting the death anxiety levels of relatives of cancer patients undergoing treatment. *Asian Pacific Journal of Cancer Prevention*, 13(5): 2405-2408.

Boulton, A. J, Vinik, A. I, Arezzo, J. C, Bril, V., Feldman, E. L, Freeman, R., Malik, R. A, Maser, R. E, Sosenko, J. M, Ziegler, D. (2005). Diabetic neuropathies: a statement by the American Diabetes Association. *Diabetes Care,* 28:956-962.

Ceretta. L.B, Reus, G.Z, Abelaira, H.M, Jornada, L.K, Schwalm, M.T, &Hoepers N.J. (2012). Increased prevalence of mood disorders and suicidal ideation in type 2 diabetic patients. *Acta Diabetol*. 49:S227-34.

Chrisma Pretorius, Stephen P. WalkerKarel G. F. Esterhuyse. (2010). Coping responses as predictors of satisfaction with life amongst a group of patients diagnosed with diabetes mellitus. *Health SA Gesondheid*15 (1), 1-5.

Copeland, K. L., Brown, J. S, &Creasman, J. M. (2012). Diabetes mellitus and sexual function in middle-aged and older women. *Obstetrics and Gynecology*. 120:331-40.

Demirtas, A., & Akbayrak, N. (2009). The adaptation to their sickness in patients with type 2 diabetes mellitus. *Anatol J Clin Investig*, 3:10–8.

Dempster, M., McCarthy, T., Davies, M. (2011). Psychological adjustment to Type 2 diabetes and relationship quality. *Diabet. Med.* 28(4), 487–492.

Depablos, D., Velasco, P., Salguero, B., Chaves, E., Mata-Poyo J, Derivas-Otero B, Garcia-Sanchez R, Viguera-Ester P. (2014). Quality of life and satisfaction with treatment in subjects with type 2 diabetes: results in Spain of the PANORAMA study. *Endocrinol Nutr*; 61: 18-26.

Diabetes Prevention Programme Research Group. (2007). Reduction in the incidence of type2 diabetes with life style interventions or metformin. *NEJM,* 346:393-403.

Dogan, R., Arslantas, D., & Unsal, A. (2015). Assessment of depression and death anxiety level in diabetic patients in Eskisehir, Turkey. *International Journal of Diabetes in Developing Countries*, 35(3):242-9.

Doruk, H., Akbay, E., Cayan, S., Bozlu, M., & Acar, D. (2005). Effect of diabetes mellitus on female sexual function and risk factors. *Arch. Androl.* 51(1), 1–6.

Ducat, L., Philipson, L. H, & Anderson, B. J. (2014). The mental health comorbidities of diabetes. *JAMA*, 312: 691–692.

Eljedi, A., Mikolajczyk, R.T., Kraemer, A, & Laaser U. (2006.) Health-related QOL in diabetic patients and controls without diabetes in refugee camps in the Gaza strip: a cross-sectional study. *BMC Public Health*, 6(1):268.

Emine, S., Kaplan, R., Serin, L., Mesude, G., Duman, R., Semra, M and Yilmaz,L. (2020). Sexual Life Quality and Marital Adjustment in Women With and Without Diabetes. *Springer*, 38:625–635

Enzlin, P., Mathieu, C., Vanderschueren, D., &Demyttenaere, K. (1998). Diabetes mellitus and female sexuality: a review of 25 years' research. *Diabet Med* 15:809–815.

Fatma, M., Ibrahim, I., Hassan, Ali., Abd, EL., Wahid, Amina Ahmed Mohamed, &Hanaa Kassem Farg (2016), Quality of Life of Type 2 Diabetic Patients in Relation to Gender and Socio-Economic Status in Egypt. *Int J Pharm Sci & Scient,* Res. 2:4, 86-94.

Fayers PM, Machin D. (2007). QOL: the assessment. Analysis and interpretation of patient-related outcomes, 2nd ed. West Sussex: John Wiley & Sons; 286-301.

Friis, A. M., Johnson, M. H., Cutfield, R. G., &Consedine, N. S. (2016). Kindness matters: a randomized controlled trial of a mindful selfcompassion intervention improves depression, distress, and HbA1c among patients with diabetes. *Diabetes Care*, 39(11), 1963–1971.

Gebremedhin, T., Workicho, A., &Angaw, D. A. (2019). Health-related quality of life and its associated factors among adult patients with type II diabetes attending MizanTepi University Teaching Hospital, Southwest Ethiopia. *BMJ Open Diabetes Research & Care*, 700-775.

Gianatti, E. J, & Grossmann, M. (2020). Testosterone deficiency in men with type 2 diabetes: Pathophysiology and treatment. *Diabetic Medicine*. 37:174-86.

Giraldi, A., & Kristensen, E. (2010). Sexual dysfunction in women with diabetes mellitus. *J. Sex. Res*. 47(2–3), 199–211.

Goebel B, & Fabbri, A. E. (2013). Eating disorders. In: Peters, A.; Laffel, L., editors. Type 1 Diabetes Sourcebook. Alexandria, VA: *American Diabetes Association*; 180-186.

Golden, S.H., Lazo, M., Carnethon, M., Bertoni, A.G., Schreiner, P.J., Diez, G., Roux, A.V, &Lyketsos, C. (2008). Examining a bidirectional association between depressive symptoms and diabetes. *Journal of the American Medical Association*, 299:2751–2759.

Goz, F., Karaoz, S., Goz, M., Ekiz, S., Cetin, I. (2007). Effects of the diabetic patients' perceived social support on their quality-of-life. *J Clin Nurs,* 16(7):1353–60.

Grandy, S., Chapman, R. H, & Fox K. M. (2008). Quality of life and depression of people living with type 2 diabetes mellitus and those at low and high risk for type 2 diabetes: findings from the Study to Help Improve Early evaluation and management of risk factors Leading to Diabetes (SHIELD). *Int J Clin Pract,* 62: 562-568.

Hamdan-Mansour A, Al Abeiat D, Alzoghaibi I, GhannamB,Hanouneh S. (2015). Psychosocial and sociodemographic correlates of life satisfaction among patients diagnosed with cancer in Jordan. *J Cancer Educ,*30:31–6.

Heinrich E, (2011). *Diabetes self-management. Strategies to support patients and health care professionals*, PhD thesis. Maastricht, The Netherlands: Maastricht University.

Ho, A. Y. K., Berggren, I., and Dahlborg-Lyckhage, E. (2010). Diabetes empowerment related to Pender's health promotion model: A meta-synthesis. *Nursing and Health Sciences*. 12: 259-267.

Jain, V., Shivkumar, S. and Gupta, O. (2014). Health-Related Quality of Life (HRQol) in Patients with Type 2 Diabetes Mellitus. *North American Journal of Medical Sciences*, 6(2), 96-101.

Jordan, D. N., Jordan, J. L. (2010). Self-care behaviors of Filipino-American adults with type 2 diabetes mellitus. *J Diabetes Complications,* 24:250–278.

Kastenbaum, R. (2007). *Death Anxiety. In Fink IG editor; Encyclopedia of Stress*. 2nd edition, Oxford: Academic Press, 717-722.

Keyhani, E., Falsafinejad, M. R, Khodabakhshi-koolaee, A . (2019). A Comparison of Marital Satisfaction and Adjustment in Diabetic and Healthy Women. *Journal of Diabetes Nursing,* 6:653-63.

Keyhani, E., Falsafinejad, M. R., Khodabakhshi-koolaee A. (2019). Comparison of Marital Satisfaction and Adjustment in Diabetic and Healthy Women. *Journal of Diabetes Nursing,*6:653-63.

Keyhani, E., Falsafinejad, M. R., Khodabakhshi-koolaee, A. (2019). Comparison of marital satisfaction and adjustment in diabetic and healthy women. *J. Diabetes Nurs*. 6(4), 653–663.

Khongsdir, S., George, C., Mukherjee, D. and Norman, G. (2015). Quality of Life in Patients with Diabetes and Hypertension in Karnataka- An Observational Study. *Int J Med Health Sci*., 4(1), 98- 102.

Kreider, K. E. (2017). Diabetes distress or major depressive disorder? A practical approach to diagnosing and treating psychological comorbidities of diabetes. *Diabetes Ther,* 8(1):1–7.

Lal, A. (2011). Bartle-Haring S. Relationship among Differentiation of Self, Relationship Satisfaction, Partner Support, and Depression in Patients with Chronic Lung Disease and Their Partners. *JMFT.* 37(2):169–81.

Lefebvre, H. &Levert, M. (2006). Sudden and unexpected health situation: From suffering to resilience. *Illness, Crisis, & Loss, 14*, 337-354.

Lustrnan, P. J., Griffith, L. S., & Clouse, R. E. (1996). *Recognizing and managing*

Madnawat, A.V., Kachhawa, P. S. (2007). Age, gender, and living circumstances: Discriminating older adults on death anxiety. *Death Stud*, 31:763-789.

Mauro, A. M. (2010). Long-term follow-up study of uncertainty and psychosocial adjustment among implantable cardioverter defibrillator recipients. *Int J Nurs Stud*,47:1080–1078.

Mikaliukstienė A, Zagminas K, & Juozulynas A, (2014). Prevalence and determinants of anxiety and depression symptoms in patients with type 2 diabetes in Lithuania. *Med Sci Monit*, 20:182–90.

Mirghafourvand M, Farshbaf-Khalili A, Ghanbari-Homayi S. (2016). The Relationship between marital adjustment and thinking styles in infertile women referred to Alzahra hospital, Tabriz -2014. *Nursing and Midwifery Journal*, 13:964-72.

Mitaw, H., Girma, L., Shambel, N., Wodajo, J., Sewunet, D., Ademe, H., Afework, K., Edmealem, Mulugeta, R., Wsilasie, L., Gebremeskel, F., &Mesafint. (2020). Health-Related Quality of Life and Associated Factors Among Type Two Diabetic Patients on Follow-Up in Dessie Comprehensive Specialized Hospital, Dessie, North East Ethiopia, 2020. Diabetes, Metabolic Syndrome and Obesity: *Targets and Therapy,* 13 4529–4541.

Mittal A, Sathian B, Kumar A, Chandrasekharan N, Sunka A. (2010). Diabetes mellitus as a Potential Risk Factor for Renal Disease among Nepalese: A Hospital Based Case Control Study. *Nepal Journal of Epidemiology*. 1(1):22-3.

Monirsadat, Z., Nematollahi, S., Roghayeh, A., Mehdipour-Rabori, Mahdieh Alinejad Dehsheakhi, and EsmatNouhi. (2020). Comparison of the Relationship Between Sexual Function, Marital Adjustmentand Life Satisfaction in Diabetic and Non-Diabetic Women. *IJCBNM*, 8(4):324-332.

Okwaraji, E., Onyebueke, G. C., Nduanya, C. U., Nwokpoku, E. N. (2017). Life Statisfaction,Self Esteem, and Mental Health in a sample of Diabetic Out-Patients Attending a Nigerian Tertiary Health Institution. *The Journal of Medical Research*, 3:60-85.

Ozkan, R., Tuncay, F., Avcı, D. (2020). Association between self-care management and life satisfaction in patients with diabetes mellitus. *European Journal of Integrative Medicine,* 35:101-199.

Ozturk, Z. A, Yesil, Y., & Kuyumcu, M. E, (2015). Association of depression and sleep quality with complications of type 2 diabetes in geriatric patients. Aging. *Clin Exp Res*, 27:533–8.

Pereira, M. G., Machado, J. C., Sousa, M. R., & Pedras, S. (2014). A study of a couple with type 2 diabetes: dyadic adjustment and psychological morbidity. Revista da AssociaçaoMédicaBrasileira 60(4), 318–326.

Pollock, S., Christian, B. and Sands, D. (1990). Responses to chronic illness: analysis of psychological and psychological adaptation. *Nursing Research,* 39(5):300-304.

Porojan, M., Poanta, L., and Dumitrascu, D. L. (2012). Assessing health related quality of life in diabetic patients Rom. *J. Intern. Med,* 50(1) 27-31.

Potes, A., Gagnon, G., Toure, E. H., & Perreault M. (2016). Patient and clinician assessments of symptomatology changes on older adults following a psychoeducational program for depression and anxiety. *Psychiatr Q* 87(4): 649-62.

Ramirez, M. J., Ferriol, E. E., Domenech, F. G., Llatas, M. C. (2003). Psychosocial adjustment in patients surgically treated for laryngeal cancer. *Otolaryngol Head Neck Surg*,129:92–107.

Reisinger, C., Walker, E., McGee, R. E. & Druss, B. G. (2015). Mortality in mental disorders and global disease burden implications: a systematic review and meta-analysis. *JAMA Psychiatry,* 72, 334–341.

Rekleiti M, Sarafis P, Saridi M, Toska A, Mellos C, Souliotis K, &TsironiM.(2013). Investigation of depression in greek patients with diabetic peripheral neuropathy. *GJHS*, 5(5):107-114.

Richard, R., & Rubin, F. (2000). Diabetes and Quality of Life. *Diabetes Spectrum*, 13:48-63.

Rogers, C. (1972). *Becoming partners: Marriage and its alternatives.* New York: Delacorte Press.

Rosiek A, Kornatowski T, Frąckowiak & Maciejewska N, (2016). Health behaviors of patients diagnosed with type 2 diabetes mellitus and their influence on the patients' satisfaction with life. *Therapeutics and Clinical Risk Management*, 12:1783-92.

Roy, T, & Lloyd, C. E. (2012). Epidemiology of depression and diabetes: a systematic review. *J Affect Disord*,142(Suppl): S8–21.

Smith, K. J., Deschenes, S. S. & Schmitz, N. (2018). Investigating the longitudinal association between diabetes and anxiety: a systematic review and meta-analysis. *Diabet. Med.* 35, 677–693.

Solli, O., Stavem, K, & Kristiansen, I. S. (2010). Health-related quality of life in diabetes: The associations of complications with EQ-5D scores. *Health and Quality of Life Outcomes*. 8:18.

Stephenson, K. R., &Meston, C. M. (2010). Differentiating components of sexual wellbeing in women: Are sexual satisfaction and sexual distress independent constructs? *J. Sex. Med.* 7(7), 2458–2468.

Tanyi, R. and Werner, J. (2003). Adjustment, spirituality and health in women on hemodialysis. *Clinical Nursing Research,*12(3):229-245.

Thapa, S., Pyakurel, P., Baral, D. D., & Jha N. (2019). Health-related quality of life among people living with type 2 diabetes: a community based cross-sectional study in rural Nepal. *BMC Public Health,*19 (1),1–6.

Trief, P., Himes, C., Orendorff, R. and Weinstock, R. (2001). The marital relationship and psychosocial adaptation and glycaemic control of individuals with diabetes. *Diabetes Care,*24:1384-1389.

Trief, P. M., Fisher, L., Sandberg, J., Hessler, D. M., Cibula, D. A., Weinstock, R. S. (2019). Research: educational and psychological aspects two for one? Effects of a couples intervention on partners of persons with Type 2 diabetes: a randomized controlled trial. *Diabet. Med.* 36, 473 –481. uterine leiomyoma and normal. *Health Research Journal,* 1(4): 207-14.

Van der Feltz-Cornelis C. M, Nuyen, J., Stoop, C., Chan, J., Jacobson, A. M., & Katon W. (2010). Sartorius N. Effect of interventions for major depressive disorder and significant depressive symptoms in patients with diabetes mellitus: A systematic review and meta-analysis. *General Hospital Psychiatry*, 32:380–395.

White, N. E., Richter, J. M., & Fry, C. (1992). Coping, social support, and adaptation to chronic illness. *Western Journal of Nursing Research*, 14(2), 211-224.

Whittemore, R. D., Eramo, T., Melkus, G., & Grey, M. (2005). Metabolic control, self-management and psychosocial adjustment in women with type 2 diabetes. *J Clin Nurs*, 14:195–203.

Willoughby, D. F., Kee, C., Demi, A. (2000). Women's psychosocial adjustment to diabetes. *J Adv Nurs,* 32:1422–1430.

Woods, N. F., Haberman, M. R., & Packard, N. J. (1993). Demands of illness and individual, dyadic, and family adaptation in chronic illness. *Western Journal of J Nursing Research*, 15(1), 10-30.

Yanikkerem, E., Goker, A., Ustgorul, S., & Karakus, A. (2016). Evaluation of sexual functions and marital adjustment of pregnant women in Turkey. *International Journal of Impotence Research*, 28:176-83.

CHAPTER – 3

METHODOLOGY

LIST OF CONTENTS

CHAPTER - 3

3 Methodology

3.1 Objectivities of the Present Research

In this chapter objective, hypotheses, sample, tools and plan of analysis have been discussed.

- To measure the impact of diabetes on mental health.
- To measure the impact of diabetes on marital adjustment.
- To measure the impact of diabetes on life satisfaction.
- To measure the impact of diabetes on adjustment.
- To measure the impact of diabetes on death anxiety.

3.2 Hypotheses

On the basis of above mentioned objectives following hypotheses were formulated:

- The mental health of non – diabetic subjects will be better than diabetic subjects.
- The marital adjustment of non – diabetic subjects will be better than diabetic subjects.
- The life satisfaction of diabetic subjects will not be better than non - diabetic subjects.
- The adjustment of non - diabetic subjects will be better than diabetic subjects.
- The death anxiety of diabetic subjects will be higher than non - diabetic subjects.

3.3 The Sample

The sample of the present study consisted of 100 diabeticand 100non - diabetic subjects (age group of 20 - 55 years) residing in Hazaribagh, Ramgarh and Ranchi district. These Data was selected by stratified random technique. The stratification was based on 2 factors of gender (male and female), and 2 factors of health status (diabeticand non - diabetic). Therefore, the research design was based on 2 x 2 factorial design and factors of stratification were:

- **Gender - 2**: Male and Female
- **Health Status - 2**:Diabeticand Non - Diabetic

Table - 3.1: Sampling Distribution

SL. No.	Gender	Diabetic	Non - Diabetic	Total
1	Male	50	50	100
2	Female	50	50	100
3	Total	100	100	200

3.3.1 Process of Sample Selection

Firstly subjects were contacted personally and briefed about the purpose of the study. Informed consent was taken prior to the administration of tools.Then participants were given the questionnaires and proper instructions for completing the questionnaires. On the fixed date, all scales were used into two sessions. In session I, Personal Data Questionnaire, PGI Health Questionnaire and Death Anxiety Scale were administered on Diabetic and non- diabetic subjects, While in session II Life Satisfaction Scale, Mohsin-Shamshad Adjustment Inventory and Marital Adjustment Questionnaire were administered on Diabetic and non-diabetic subjects.

Inclusion Criteria

- Mentally normal subjects were included.
- Only age 20 to 50 years subjects were included.
- Only married subjects were included.
- Hindi knowing subjects were included.

Exclusion Criteria

- The subjects suffering from chronic diseases like AIDS, Hepatitis – B, Cancer were excluded.
- The married subjects below age 20 years and above 50 years were excluded.
- Subjects who were physically handicapped.

3.4 Tools to be used in Collection of Data

The following tools used for the data collection:

3.4.1 Personal Data Questionnaire (PDQ)

3.4.2 PGI Health Questionnaire (PGI HQ)

3.4.3 Marital Adjustment Questionnaire (MAQ)

3.4.4 Life Satisfaction Scale (LSS)

3.4.5 Mohsin-Shamshad Adjustment Inventory (MSAI)

3.4.6 Death Anxiety Scale (DAS)

3.4.1 Personal Data Questionnaire (PDQ)

Personal Data Questionnaire was prepared by the researcher. This elicited respondent's basic information, such as name, age, gender, level of education, place of residence etc.

3.4.2 PGI Health Questionnaire (PGI HQ)

This questionnaire was developed by Verma, Wig & Prasad (1985). This test is useful not only for clinical work in screening and assessing the progress of treatment but has a larger utility in clinical psychiatric research. It is a short, simple test with low difficulty value for items and it can be used with illiterate, unsophisticated population also. Higher score usually indicates greater chances of developing psychiatric symptoms.

Reliability: Reliability of the test was examined using 'test-retest' and 'split-half' method and was found to be significantly high (0.88 & 0.86respectively).

Validity: Validity of PGI HQ N-1 was established administering other well-known test of neuroticism concomitantly. It was found that the total score of the PGI HQ N-1 was highly correlates with similar traits of other scale. Separate scores of section "A" and "B" were found relatively lower correlation (though still significant) with measures of neuroticism another tests. This confirms that a combined of physical and psychological scores constitutes a better measure of neuroticism. If one obtains high scores only on one of the two sections, then there are relatively less chances of his being accuse of neurosis. The test was cross validated on fresh sample from Chandigarh. Ahmadabad and Rohtak. It was found that mean scores of male & female psychiatric patients were comparable but were comparable but were markedly distinct from normal.

3.4.3 Marital Adjustment Questionnaire (MAQ)

This questionnaire was developed by Pramod Kumar and Kanchana Rohatgi). This was used to access the marital adjustment among the married couples. This questionnaire consists of 25 items, out of which 22 items are positive and 3 items are negative. There are two response alternative for each item :Yes and No. for positive items, score is 1 and 0 is given respectively and vice-versa for the negative items. Negatives items are 4, 10, and 19. Except these three items all are positive items. The sum of all 25 items gives overall marital adjustment scores. Thus range of scores is 0 to 25. Higher scores, shows better the marital adjustment and vice-versa. Reliability of this scale is 0.75 and validity is reported 0.78.

3.4.3 Life Satisfaction Scale (LSS)

This scale was designed and developed by Q.G. Alam & Dr. Ramji Srivastava (2001). Published by National psychological corporation, Agra. The L.S.S. comprises of 60 items related to six areas of life viz. Health, Personal, Economic, Marital, Social and Job. The responses are to given in yes/no. yes responses indicate Satisfaction, whereas No indicate Dissatisfaction.

Test-Retest reliability quotient is 0.84. The validity of the scale was obtained by correlating it with Saxon's Adjustment Inventory and Srivastava adjustment inventory. The quotient obtained was 0.74and 0.84 respectively.

3.4.4 Mohsin-Shamshad Adjustment Inventory (MSAI)

This inventory was used to measure the adjustment of the subject. It is Hindi adaptation of bell adjustment inventory. It was modified in 1987.This inventory is consists of 124 items, which measure adjustment, four dimension namely, Home, health, social and emotional.

The reliability of this scale is .75 to .89 and the validity of the scale is .58 to .89.

3.4.5 Death Anxiety Scale (DAS)

This scale was developed by G.P. Thakur and Manju Thakur (1983). This scale had sixteen statements. Statement numbers, 1,2,4,5,7,9,10,12,13,15 and 16 were positively worded and numbers 3,6,8,11 and 14 were negatively worded. Responses on the positively worded statement would get 5,4,3,2 and 1 for the "quite true", "true", "Undecided", "false" and "quite true", "true", "Undecided", "false" and "quite false" response categories. The maximum score, one could get on the scale, would be 80 and the minimum would be 16.

Reliability:

The death anxiety scale was administered on a sample of 206 Indians of both the sexes for ascertaining reliability co-efficient. Internal consistency reliability co-efficient using Kuder-Richardson formula was found to be 0.78 and a test retest reliability co-efficient with a gap of about twelve weeks on 65 Ss was 0.86. The reliability co-efficient, therefore, were considered satisfactory.

Validity:

With a view to ascertaining validity co-efficient of the death anxiety scale, the scale along with the Templar's scale of the CPS, there scales-Trust (T), Activity (A) and Extroversion (E) had negative relationship with the Thakur Death anxiety scale (TDAS). Other five scales - orderliness (O), Social conformity (C), emotional stability (S), Masculinity (M) and Empathy (P) had positive relationship with the TDAS in greater or smaller degree.

3.5 Plan of Analysis

The statistical analysis was done with the help of Statistical package for Social Science-20 (SPSS-20) and used t test.

3.5 References

Donovan, N., & Halpern, D. (2002). Life satisfaction: the state of knowledge and implications for government. Retrieved online on Sep 12, 2011fromhttp://www.cabinetoffice.gov.uk/media/cabinetoffice/strategy/assets/paper.pdf.

Lambert, E. G., Hogan, N. L., Elechi, O. O., Jiang, S., Laux, J. M., Dupuy, P. & Morris, A. (2009). A further examination of antecedents of correctional staff life satisfaction. *The Social Science Journal,* 46, 689-706.

Lewis, V., & Borders, L. (1995). Life satisfaction of single middle-aged professional women. *Journal of Counselling and Development,* 74, 94-100.

Veenhoven, R. (1996). The study of life satisfaction. In W.E.Saris, R. Veenhoven, A.C. Scherpenzeel, & B. Bunting (Eds.), *A comparative study of satisfaction with life in Europe* (pp.11-48). Budapest: Eotvos University Press.

CHAPTER – 4

Results and Discussion

LIST OF CONTENTS

CHAPTER – 4

4 Results and Discussion

In this chapter the results are presented under the following heads:

4.1. The impact of diabetes on mental health.

4.2. The impact of diabetes on marital adjustment.

4.3. The impact of diabetes on life satisfaction.

4.4. The impact of diabetes on adjustment.

4.5. The impact of diabetes on death anxiety.

4.1 The Impact of Diabetes on Mental Health

The mean scores, SD and t value of diabetic and non - diabetic subjects on mental health are presented in table 4.1and mean scores are show in figure 4.1.The results revealed that:

Table 4.1

N, Mean, SD and t-Value of Diabetic and Non - Diabetic on Mental Health

Total	N	Mean	SD	t value	P
Diabetic	100	14.81	2.14	3.32	0.01*
Non - Diabetic	100	13.80	2.34		

* Significant on 0.01 level

- The mean scores of diabetic and non- diabetic subjects on mental health were 14.81 and 13.80 respectively. The difference between mean scores of diabetic and non- diabetic subject was 1.01 and t value was 3.32 which was statistically significant at 0.01 level. This indicated that diabetic subjects had significantly high mental health than non-diabetic subjects.

Hence, the hypothesis stating that the mental health of non – diabetic subjects will be better than diabetic subjects is rejected.

Figure: 4.1

Comparison between Diabetic and Non-Diabetic on their Mean of Mental Health

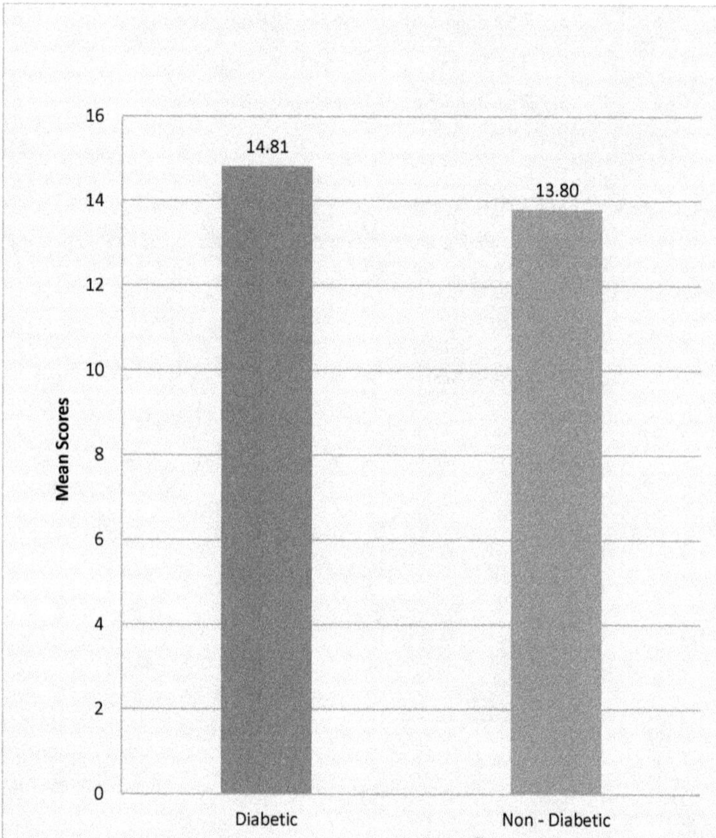

4.1.1 The Impact of Diabetes on Mental Health among Male Subjects

The mean scores, SD and t value of diabetic and non - diabetic male subjects on mental health are presented in table 4.2 and mean scores are show in figure 4.2. The results revealed that:

Table 4.2

N, Mean, SD and t-Value of Male Diabetic and Non - Diabetic on Mental Health

Total	N	Mean	SD	t	P
Diabetic	50	14.62	2.12	1.98	0.05*
Non - Diabetic	50	13.66	2.66		

* Significant on 0.05 level

- The mean scores of male diabetic and male non- diabetic subjects on mental health were 14.62 and 13.66 respectively. The difference between mean scores of male diabetic and non- diabetic subject was 0.96 and t value was 1.98 which was statistically significant at 0.05 level. This indicated that male diabetic subjects had significantly high mental health than male non- diabetic subjects.

Hence, the hypothesis stating that the mental health of non – diabetic subjects will be better than diabetic subjects is rejected in relation to male diabetic and non- diabetic subjects.

Figure: 4.2

Comparison between Male Diabetic and Non-Diabetic on their Mean of Mental Health

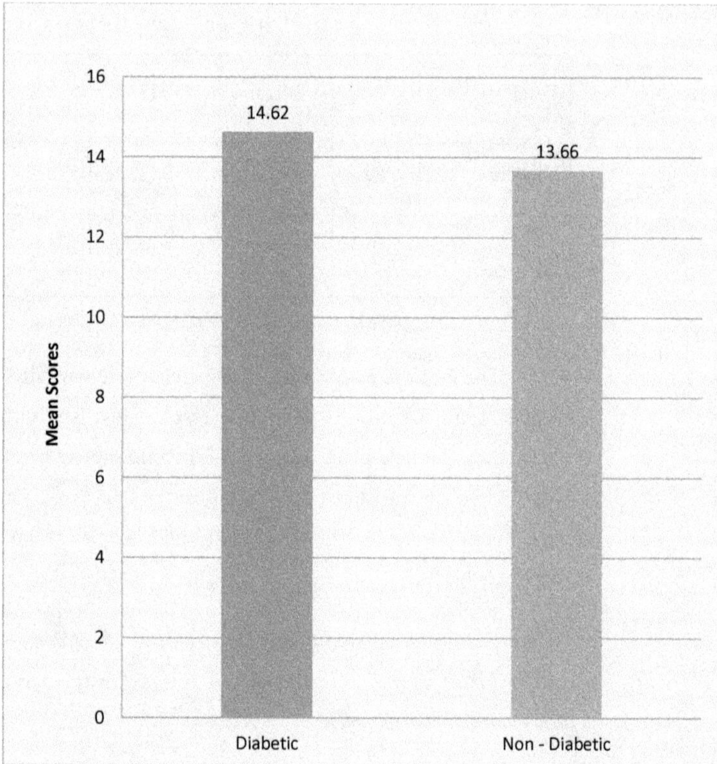

4.1.2 The Impact of Diabetes on Mental Health among Female Subjects

The mean scores, SD and t value of diabetic and non – diabetic female subjects on mental health are presented in table 4.3and mean scores are show in figure 4.3. The results revealed that:

Table 4.3

N, Mean, SD and t-Value of Female Diabetic and Non - Diabetic on Mental Health

Total	N	Mean	SD	t	P
Diabetic	50	15	2.17	2.70	0.01
Non - Diabetic	50	13.80	2		

* Significant on 0.01 level

- The mean scores of female diabetic and female non- diabetic subjects on mental health were 15 and 13.80 respectively. The difference between mean scores of female diabetic and non- diabetic subject was 1.20 and t value was 2.70 which was statistically significant at 0.01 level. This indicated that female diabetic subjects had significantly high mental health than female non-diabetic subjects.

Hence, the hypothesis stating that the mental health of non – diabetic subjects will be better than diabetic subjects is rejected in relation to female diabetic and non- diabetic subjects.

Figure: 4.3

Comparison between Male Female Diabetic and Non-Diabetic on their Mean of Mental Health

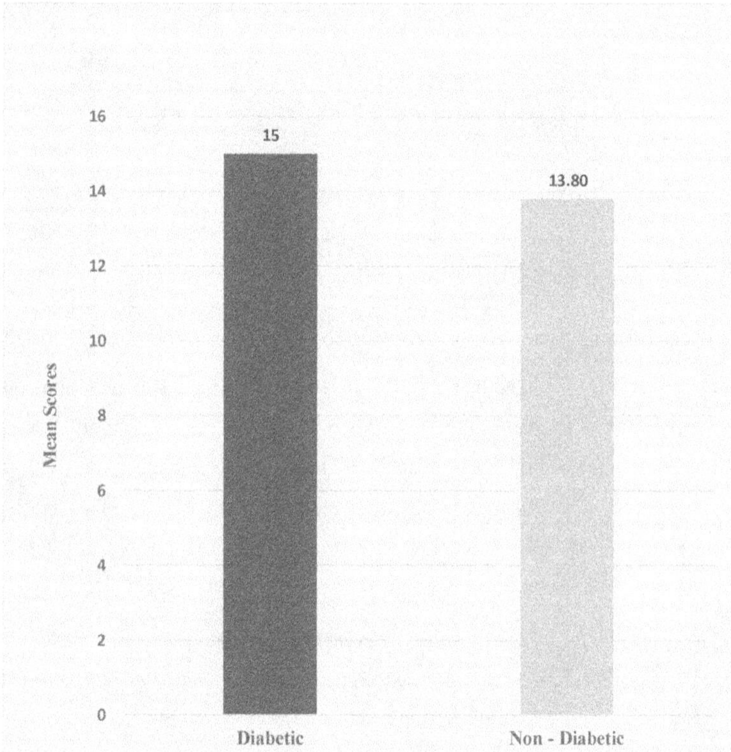

4.2 The Impact of Diabetes on Death Anxiety

The mean scores, SD and t value of diabetic and non - diabetic subjects on death anxiety are presented in table 4.4 and mean scores are show in figure 4.4. The results revealed that:

Table 4.4

N, Mean, SD and t-Value of Diabetic and Non - Diabetic on Death Anxiety

Total	N	Mean	SD	t	P
Diabetic	100	53.78	7.08	1.73	NS*
Non - Diabetic	100	52.23	5.12		

* NS = Significant

- The mean scores of diabetic and non- diabetic subjects on death anxiety were 53.78 and 52.23 respectively. The difference between mean scores of diabetic and non- diabetic subject was 1.55 and t value was 1.73. This value was statistically not significant. This indicated that diabetic and non- diabetic subjects did not differ significantly on death anxiety.

Hence, the hypothesis stating that the death anxiety of diabetic subjects will be higher than non - diabetic subjects is accepted.

Figure: 4.4

Comparison between Diabetic and Non-Diabetic on their Mean of Death Anxiety

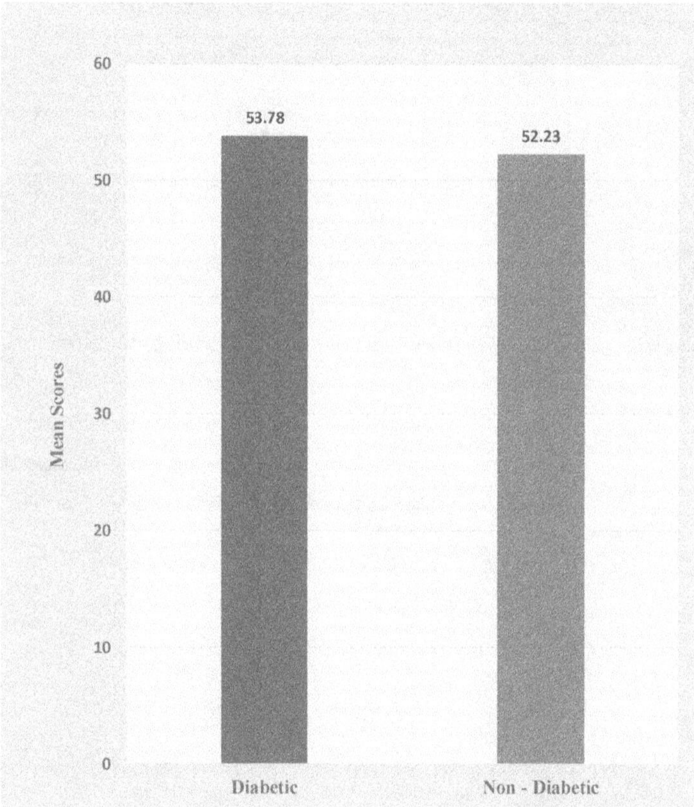

4.2.1 The Impact of Diabetes on Death Anxiety among Male Subjects

The mean scores, SD and t value of diabetic and non - diabetic male subjects on death anxiety are presented in table 4.5and mean scores are show in figure 4.5. The results revealed that:

Table 4.5

N, Mean, SD and t-Value of Male Diabetic and Non - Diabetic on Death Anxiety

Total	N	Mean	SD	t	P
Diabetic	50	53.94	7.71	1.6	NS*
Non - Diabetic	50	51.86	5.03		

*NS = Not Significant

- The mean scores of male diabetic and male non- diabetic subjects on death anxiety were 53.94 and 51.86 respectively. The difference between mean scores of male diabetic and non- diabetic subject was 2.08 and t value was 1.60. This value was statistically not significant. This indicated that diabetic and non - diabetic subjects did not differ significantly on death anxiety.

Hence, the hypothesis stating that the death anxiety of diabetic subjects will be higher than non - diabetic subjects is accepted in relation to male subjects.

Figure: 4.5

Comparison between Male Diabetic and Non-Diabetic on their Mean of Death Anxiety

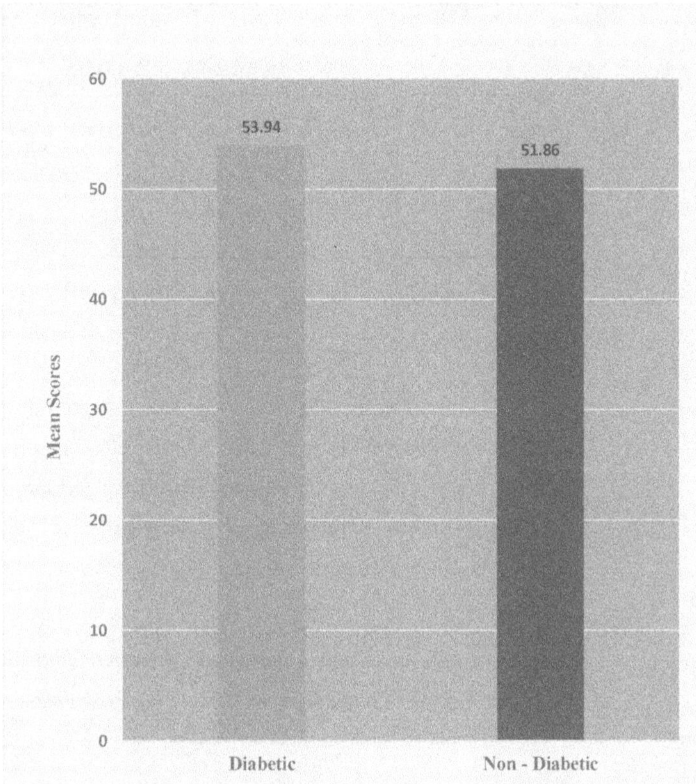

4.2.2 The Impact of Diabetes on Death Anxiety among Female Subjects

The mean scores, SD and t value of diabetic and non - diabetic female subjects on death anxiety are presented in table 4.6and mean scores are show in figure 4.6. The results revealed that:

Table 4.6

N, Mean, SD and t-Value of Female Diabetic and Non - Diabetic on Death Anxiety

Total	N	Mean	SD	t	P
Diabetic	50	53.62	6.46	2.70	0.01*
Non - Diabetic	50	50.84	2.69		

*Significant on 0.01 level

- The mean scores of female diabetic and female non- diabetic subjects on death anxiety were 53.62 and 50.84 respectively. The difference between mean scores of female diabetic and non- diabetic subject was 2.78 and t value was 2.70. which was statistically significant at 0.01 level. This indicated that female diabetic subjects had significantly high death anxiety than female non-diabetic subjects.

Hence, the hypothesis stating that the death anxiety of diabetic subjects will be higher than non - diabetic subjects is accepted in relation to female subjects.

Figure: 4.6

Comparison between Female Diabetic and Non-Diabetic on their Mean of Death Anxiety

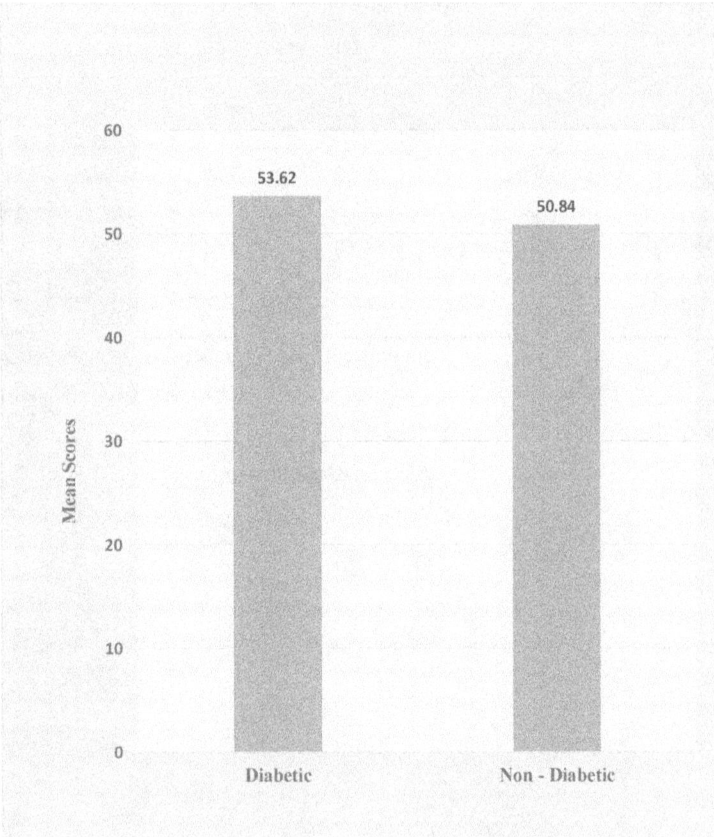

4.3 The Impact of Diabetes on Life Satisfaction

The mean scores, SD and t value of diabetic and non - diabetic subjects on life satisfaction are presented in table 4.7and mean scores are show in figure 4.7. The results revealed that:

Table 4.7

N, Mean, SD and t-Value of Diabetic and Non - Diabetic on Life Satisfaction

Total	N	Mean	SD	t	P
Diabetic	100	40.53	6.08	1.86	NS*
Non - Diabetic	100	39.13	4.87		

* NS = Significant

- The mean scores of diabetic and non- diabetic subjects on lifesatisfaction were 40.53 and 39.13 respectively. The difference between mean scores of diabetic and non- diabetic subject was 1.40 and t value was 1.86. This value was statistically not significant. This indicated that diabetic and non - diabetic subjects did not differ significantly on life satisfaction.

Hence, the hypothesis stating that the life satisfaction of diabetic subjects will not be better than non - diabetic subjects is rejected.

Figure: 4.7

Comparison between Diabetic and Non-Diabetic on their Mean of Life Satisfaction

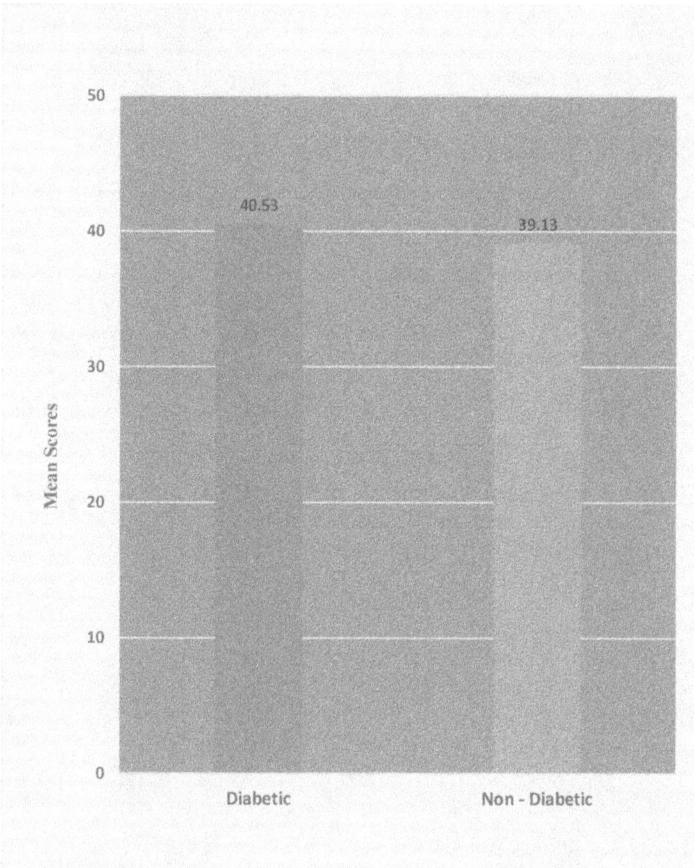

4.3.1 The Impact of Diabetes on Life Satisfaction among Male Subjects

The mean scores, SD and t value of diabetic and non – diabetic male subjects on life satisfaction are presented in table 4.8and mean scores are show in figure 4.8. The results revealed that:

Table 4.8

N, Mean, SD and t-Value of Male Diabetic and Non - Diabetic on Life Satisfaction

Total	N	Mean	SD	t	P
Diabetic	50	40.34	5.99	1.63	NS*
Non - Diabetic	50	38.72	4.17		

* NS = Significant

- The mean scores of male diabetic and male non- diabetic subjects on lifesatisfaction were 40.34 and 38.72 respectively. The difference between mean scores of male diabetic and non- diabetic subject was 1.62 and t value was 1.63. This value was statistically not significant. This indicated that diabetic and non - diabetic subjects did not differ significantly on life satisfaction.

Hence, the hypothesis stating that the life satisfaction of diabetic subjects will not be better than non - diabetic subjects is rejected in relation to male subjects.

Figure: 4.8

Comparison between Male Diabetic and Non-Diabetic on their Mean of Life Satisfaction

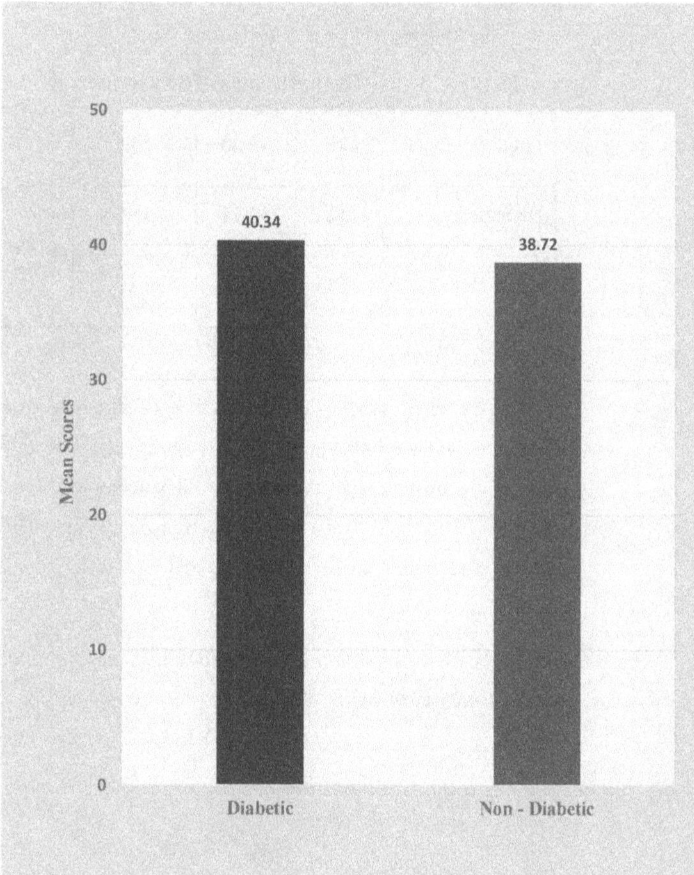

4.3.2 The Impact of Diabetes on Life Satisfaction among Female Subjects

The mean scores, SD and t value of diabetic and non - diabetic female subjects on life satisfaction are presented in table 4.9and mean scores are show in figure 4.9. The results revealed that:

Table 4.9

N, Mean, SD and t-Value of Female Diabetic and Non - Diabetic on Life Satisfaction

Total	N	Mean	SD	t	P
Diabetic	50	40.72	6.23	1.27	NS*
Non - Diabetic	50	39.26	5.46		

* NS = Significant

- The mean scores of female diabetic and female non- diabetic subjects on lifesatisfaction were 40.72 and 39.26 respectively. The difference between mean scores of female diabetic and non- diabetic subject was 1.46 and t value was 1.27. This value was statistically not significant. This indicated that diabetic and non - diabetic subjects did not differ significantly on life satisfaction.

Hence, the hypothesis stating that the life satisfaction of diabetic subjects will not be better than non - diabetic subjects is rejected in relation to female subjects.

Figure: 4.9

Comparison between Female Diabetic and Non-Diabetic on their Mean of Life Satisfaction

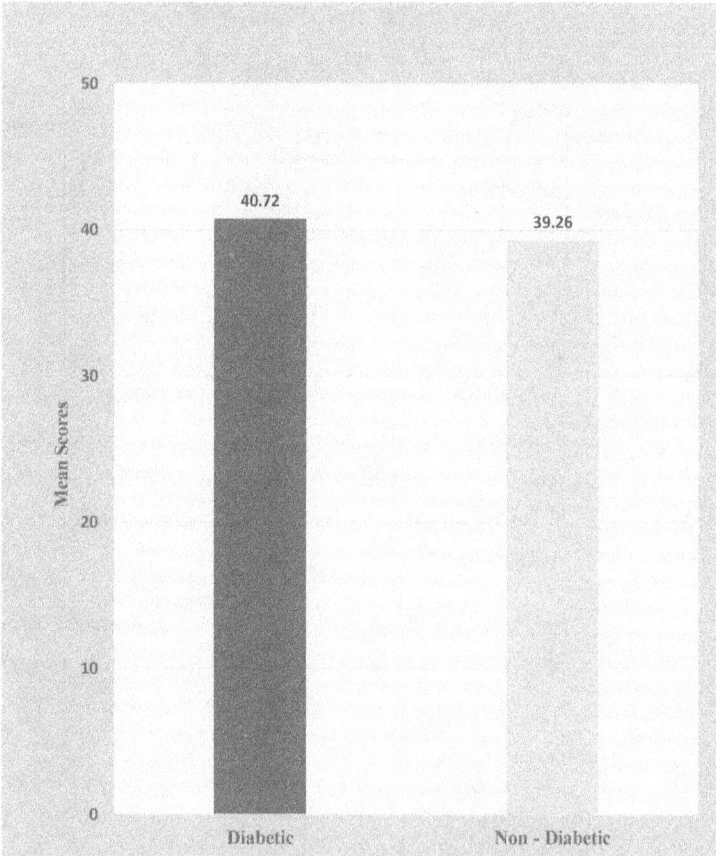

4.4 The Impact of Diabetes on Adjustment

The mean scores, SD and t value of diabetic and non - diabetic subjects on adjustment are presented in table 4.10and mean scores are show in figure 4.10. The results revealed that:

Table 4.10

N, Mean, SD and t-Value of Diabetic and Non - Diabetic on Adjustment

Total	N	Mean	SD	t	P
Diabetic	100	58.74	7.21	2.7	NS*
Non - Diabetic	100	55.46	9.41		

* NS = Significant

- The mean scores of diabetic and non- diabetic subjects on adjustment were 58.74 and 55.46 respectively. The difference between mean scores of diabetic and non- diabetic subject was 3.28 and t value was 2.70. This value was statistically not significant. This indicated that diabetic and non - diabetic subjects did not differ significantly on adjustment.

Hence, the hypothesis stating that the adjustment of non - diabetic subjects will be better than diabetic subjects is rejected.

Figure: 4.10

Comparison between Diabetic and Non-Diabetic on their Mean of Adjustment

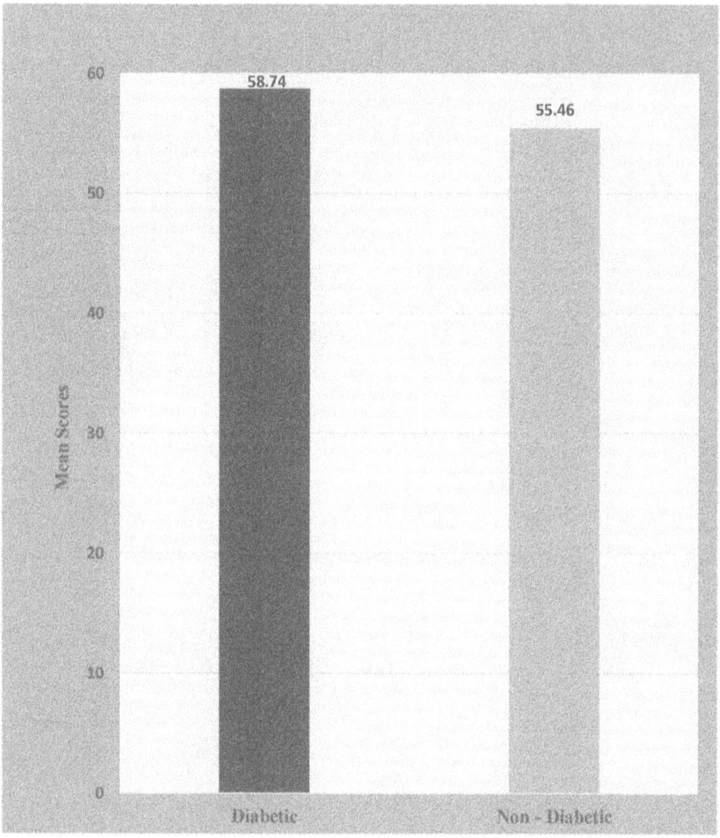

4.4.1 The Impact of Diabetes on Adjustment among Male Subjects

The mean scores, SD and t value of diabetic and non - diabetic male subjects on adjustment are presented in table 4.11and mean scores are show in figure 4.11. The results revealed that:

Table 4.11

N, Mean, SD and t-Value of Male Diabetic and Non - Diabetic on Adjustment

Total	N	Mean	SD	t	P
Diabetic	50	55.22	6.48	1.92	NS*
Non - Diabetic	50	51.74	9.67		

NS = Significant

- The mean scores of male diabetic and male non- diabetic subjects on adjustment were 55.22 and 51.74 respectively. The difference between mean scores of male diabetic and non- diabetic subject was 3.48 and t value was 1.92. This value was statistically not significant. This indicated that diabetic and non - diabetic subjects did not differ significantly on adjustment.

Hence, the hypothesis stating that the adjustment of non - diabetic subjects will be better than diabetic subjects is rejected in relation to male subjects.

Figure: 4.11

Comparison between Male Diabetic and Non-Diabetic on their Mean of Adjustment

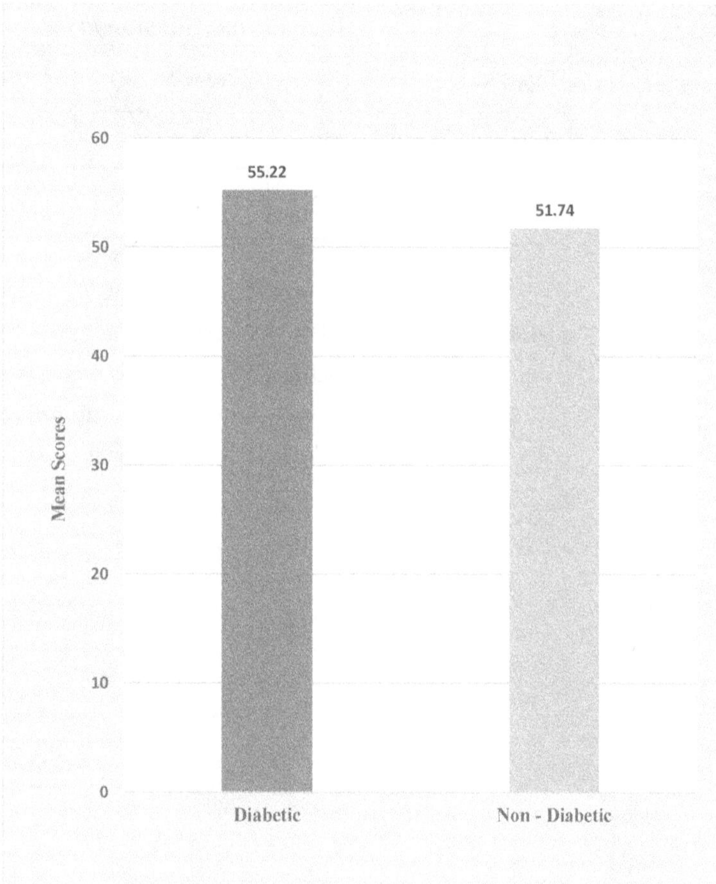

4.4.2 The Impact of Diabetes on Adjustment among Female Subjects

The mean scores, SD and t value of diabetic and non - diabetic female subjects on adjustment are presented in table 4.12and mean scores are show in figure 4.12. The results revealed that:

Table 4.12

N, Mean, SD and t-Value of Female Diabetic and Non - Diabetic on Adjustment

Total	N	Mean	SD	t	P
Diabetic	50	62.26	6.14	3.08	0.01*
Non - Diabetic	50	59.18	7.55		

* Significant on 0.01

- The mean scores of female diabetic and female non- diabetic subjects on adjustment were 62.26 and 59.18 respectively. The difference between mean scores of female diabetic and non- diabetic subject was 3.08 and t value was 3.08. which was statistically significant at 0.01 level. This indicated that female diabetic subjects had significantly high adjustment than female non-diabetic subjects.

Hence, the hypothesis stating that the adjustment of non - diabetic subjects will be better than diabetic subjects is rejected in relation to female subjects.

Figure: 4.12

Comparison between Female Diabetic and Non-Diabetic on their Mean of Adjustment

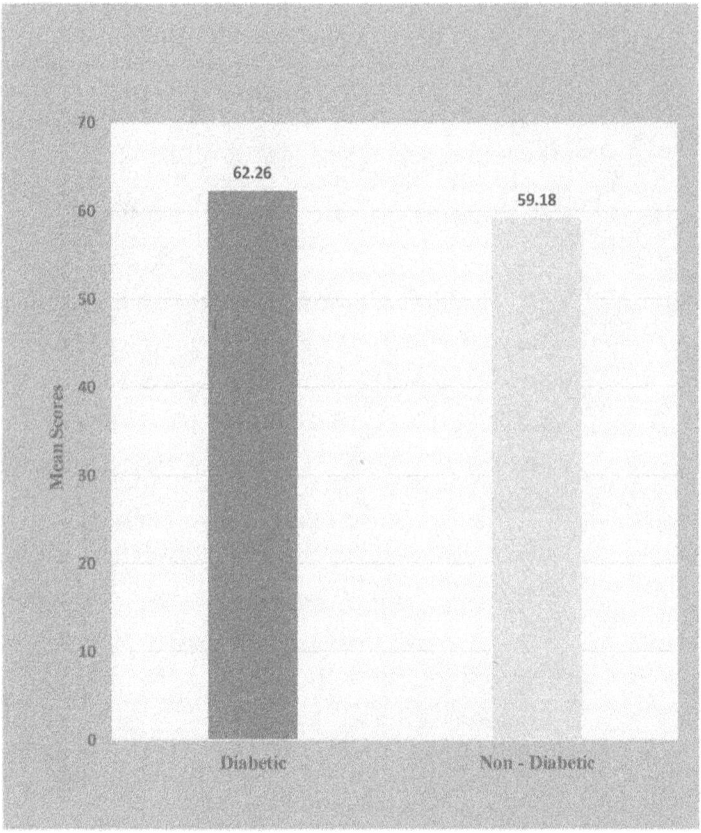

4.5 The Impact of Diabetes on Marital Adjustment

The mean scores, SD and t value of diabetic and non - diabetic subjects on marital adjustment are presented in table 4.13 and mean scores are show in figure 4.13. The results revealed that:

Table 4.13

N, Mean, SD and t-Value of Diabetic and Non - Diabetic on Marital Adjustment

Total	N	Mean	SD	t	P
Diabetic	100	50.20	3.08	5.57	0.01*
Non - Diabetic	100	45.89	7.1		

* Significant on 0.01 level

- The mean scores of diabetic and non- diabetic subjects on marital adjustment were 50.20 and 45.89 respectively. The difference between mean scores of diabetic and non- diabetic subject was 4.31 and t value was 5.57. which was statistically significant at 0.01 level. This indicated that diabetic subjects had significantly high marital adjustment than non-diabetic subjects.

Hence, the hypothesis stating that the marital adjustment of non – diabetic subjects will be better than diabetic subjects is rejected.

Figure: 4.13

Comparison between Diabetic and Non-Diabetic on their Mean of Marital Adjustment

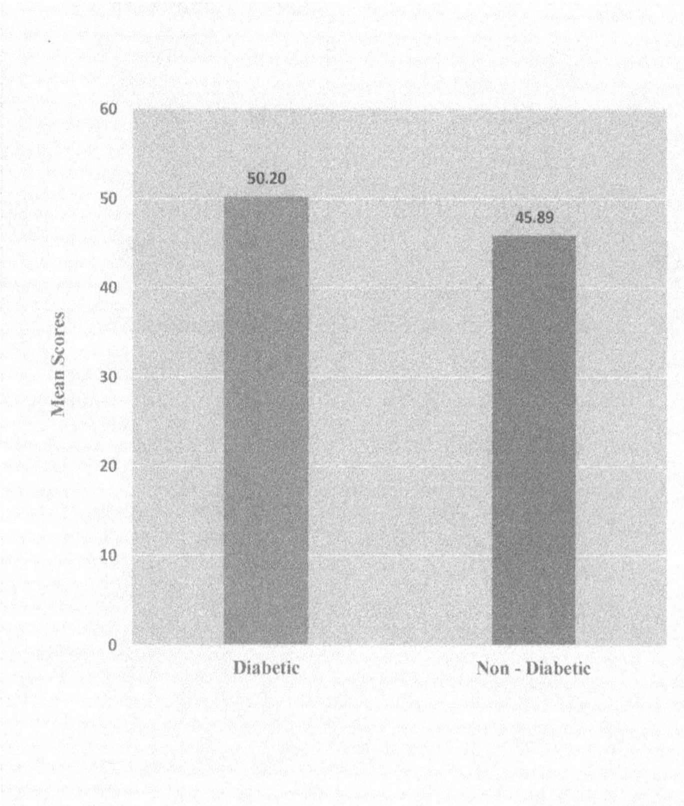

4.5.1. The Impact of Diabetes on Marital Adjustment among Male Subjects

The mean scores, SD and t value of diabetic and non - diabetic male subjects on marital adjustment are presented in table 4.14 and mean scores are show in figure 4.14. The results revealed that:

Table 4.14

N, Mean, SD and t-Value of Male Diabetic and Non - Diabetic on Marital Adjustment

Total	N	Mean	SD	t	P
Diabetic	50	50.08	2.61	4.17	0.01*
Non - Diabetic	50	44.6	8.74		

* Significant on 0.01 level

- The mean scores of male diabetic and male non- diabetic subjects on marital adjustment were 50.08 and 44.60 respectively. The difference between mean scores of male diabetic and non- diabetic subject was 5.48 and t value was 4.17. which was statistically significant at 0.01 level. This indicated that male diabetic subjects had significantly high marital adjustment than male non-diabetic subjects.

Hence, the hypothesis stating that the marital adjustment of non – diabetic subjects will be better than diabetic subjects is rejected in relation to male subjects.

Figure: 4.14

Comparison between Male Diabetic and Non-Diabetic on their Mean of Marital Adjustment

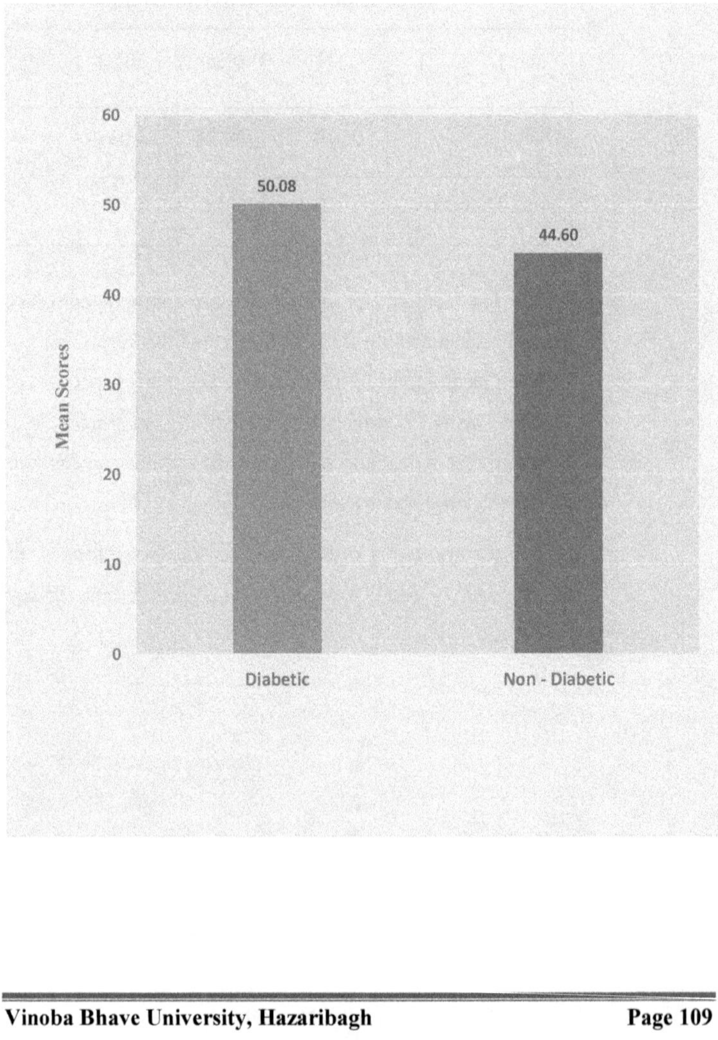

4.5.2. The Impact of Diabetes on Marital Adjustment among Female Subjects

The mean scores, SD and t value of diabetic and non - diabetic female subjects on marital adjustment are presented in table 4.15and mean scores are show in figure 4.15. The results revealed that:

Table 4.15

N, Mean, SD and t-Value of Female Diabetic and Non - Diabetic on Marital Adjustment

Total	N	Mean	SD	t	P
Diabetic	50	50.02	3.5	3.95	0.01*
Non - Diabetic	50	47.18	4.7		

* Significant on 0.01 level

- The mean scores of female diabetic and female non- diabetic subjects on marital adjustment were 50.02 and 47.18 respectively. The difference between mean scores of female diabetic and non- diabetic subject was 2.84 and t value was 3.95. which was statistically significant at 0.01 level. This indicated that female diabetic subjects had significantly high marital adjustment than female non-diabetic subjects.

Hence, the hypothesis stating that the marital adjustment of non – diabetic subjects will be better than diabetic subjects is rejected in relation to female subjects.

Figure: 4.15

Comparison between Female Diabetic and Non-Diabetic on their Mean of Marital Adjustment

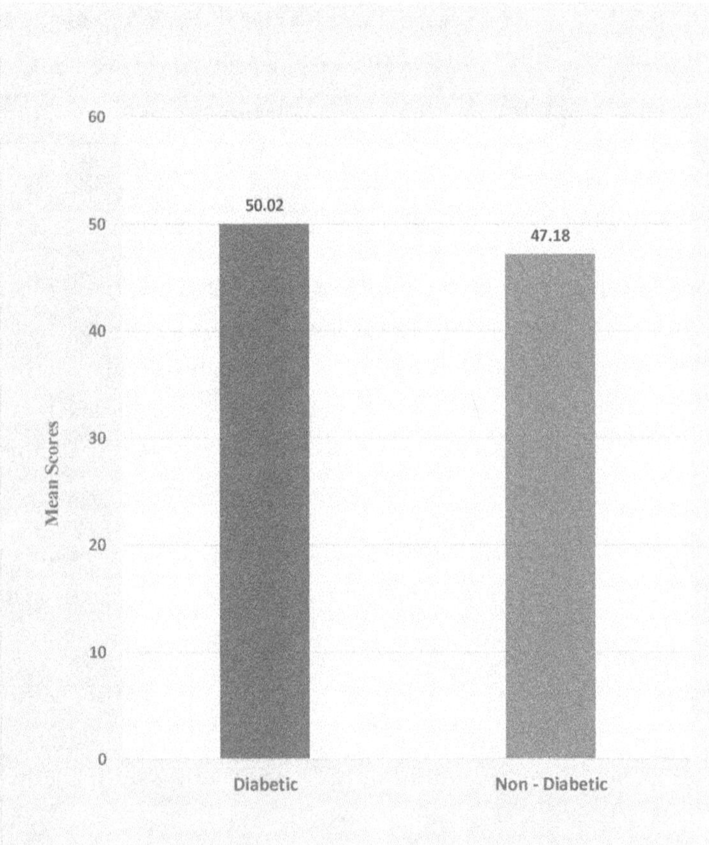

4.6 Discussion

4.6.1 Diabetic patient have better mental health compared to non-diabetic subject

The diagnosis of type 1 diabetes increases the risk by two- to threefold for comorbid mental health conditions, in particular depression, anxiety disorders, and eating disorders.(de Groot 2014) As well as diabetes distress. Mental health disorders affect more than 80 million Americans and disrupt their ability to cope with activities of daily life. When psychiatric disorders are not treated in individuals without type 1 diabetes, the individual, family, and societal costs are staggering and include disability, unemployment, family dysfunction, homelessness, substance abuse, incarceration, and suicide.(Outlook 2014) When mental health co morbidities of diabetes are not diagnosed and treated in individuals with type 1 diabetes, the financial cost to society and health care systems is even more catastrophic and the individual and family suffering that results is even more severe.(Egede, Zheng and Simpson, 2002).

Therefore, we can say that If the state spend more on the awareness, early detection, and publish some form of recommendation and dietary patterns for the Diabetic patients. Then it may certainly lead to the balance or somewhere better mental condition of the person suffering from diabetes then person who is non diabetic.

4.6.2 Diabetic and non-diabetic subjects are not different on death anxiety

Several factors were responsible behind this phenomenon. Most of the samples were more than 50 years old. They were almost free from their domestic responsibility. That is why diabetic and non-diabetic persons did not differ on death anxiety. Next measure cause behind this finding was freedom from settlement. Almost all sample were selected settled in Hazaribag district. They had their own house and there was no tension for livelihood. They had shed their own burden, which may produce anxiety. That is why the subjects did not varied on death anxiety. The next cause was settlement of their dependents and marriage of their children. The sample in this research has married their daughter, which is the main cause of anxiety with ultimate converts in death. The next important cause behind this finding is high level of religiosity of the sample. The samples were highly religious. Researches has proved that highly religious person have less death anxiety. Some sample was from Christian and Muslim communities, which has less death anxiety in comparison to other religious persons.

4.6.3 Diabetic and non- diabetic subjects are not different on life satisfaction

Spousal relationships are influenced by events, circumstances, and interactions within couples 'fives (Spanier, 1979). Referred to dyadic adjustment as a process rather than an unchanging state. (Schafer and Kelth, 1984) Postulated that the way marriage partners perceive their spouses' feelings about them may determine how couples approach and perform marital roles, interact with each other, and evaluate their marital relationship. A positive perception by marriage partners of each other contributes to the positive evaluation of the marital relationship. Simmons and Ball (1984). reported that women married to men who were disabled prior to marriage had significantly better marital adjustment than those who were married prior to the disabling injury (Petroni,1969). reported that wives were more instrumental in influencing the illness behavior of their husbands than vice versa. Katz, (1969) studied the interaction of women with husbands who had diabetes. The women discussed the frequency and severity of their unhappiness and the repetition of problems in their marriages. Conflicts within the marriage were often acted out through the medium of diabetes. Most of the women felt that the problems of diabetes infiltrated their everyday life. Another source of contlict was the 'doublebind' situation that is, being over protective versus becoming indifferent to the husband's lack of compliance. Thus a couple may use the regimen of diabetes as a vehicle for acting out inner conflicts. Conversely. support from the family and spouse may reduce the stress associated with diabetes. Highly supported persons have been reported to be more compliant in taking medications than person receiving low support. .

4.6.4 Diabetic patient have better marital adjustment compared to non diabetic patient

The influence of marital support may be particularly significant, as the diabetes care regimen (e.g. food purchase and preparation, medication administration, and exercise involvement) often involves spouses. (Coyne, Smith, 1984.) Studies have shown that spouse involvement in diabetes education programs improves outcomes. (Glidden and Wing, 1991.) Whereas spouse criticality relates to poorer blood glucose control (Klausner, 1995.) Recent studies of our group have focused on the relationship between marital variables and diabetes related outcomes. To better understand the nature of marital support, we interviewed patients with diabetes and their spouses and asked them to define those behaviors and attitudes they found helpful or not helpful for their efforts to maintain a healthy diabetes care regimen.(Trief,2003.) This qualitative look at couples living with diabetes highlighted the important role that the spouse can play in helping the individual with diabetes maintain his or her commitment to the self-management regimen, as well as the high likelihood, and negative effect, of marital conflict. In a quantitative study of 78 insulin-treated adults, we found that marital quality related to, and 2 years later prospectively predicted, both diabetes-specific and general quality of life, suggesting that marital adjustment is an important factor contributing to adaptation to the disease. There was also a non significant trend for marital adjustment scores to relate to blood glucose control but this relationship was not demonstrated in the prospective analyses. (Trief and Himes, 2001.) In our study, we hypothesized that better marital quality would also relate to regimen adherence and that this relationship would be maintained in prospective analyses.

4.6.5 Diabetic and non- diabetic subjects are not different on adjustment

It is a common feature in chronic diseases like diabetes that patients must keep up with their care in order to keep their condition under control. progression is to the disease is made up of improvements in healthcare, family structure, intimate relationships, home life, and social networks, as well as well as of transition to the environment. The adjustment to diabetes is determined by several variables unique to the condition, care, and by each patient as a person. It is made up of such variables as the patient's view of their wellbeing and the impact of the disease on it, gender, age, and duration of the condition on different professions. Assessing one's glucose levels and maintaining a specific blood glucose goal rather than simply not going over and below them as much as possible (Pollock 1990). Understanding the human variables that impact the extent to which one's metabolism will influence one's degree of responsiveness to the disease would allow for the discovery of potential prevention measures to be followed.

White (1992) published research on female diabetes adaptation. This study showed that the health and psychosocial effects were similar regardless of whether a woman suffered with a chronic disease for a short or long.

4.7 Main Findings

- Diabetic subjects had significantly high mental health than non-diabetic subjects.
- Male diabetic subjects had significantly high mental health than male non diabeticsubjects.
- Female diabetic subjects had significantly high mental health than female nondiabetic subjects.
- Diabetic and non- diabetic subjects did not differ significantly on death anxiety.
- Male diabetic and non - diabetic subjects did not differ significantly on deathanxiety.
- Female diabetic subjects had significantly high death anxiety than female nondiabetic subjects.
- Diabetic and non - diabetic subjects did not differ significantly on life satisfaction.
- Male diabetic and non - diabetic subjects did not differ significantly on lifesatisfaction.
- Female diabetic and non - diabetic subjects did not differ significantly on lifesatisfaction.
- Diabetic and non - diabetic subjects did not differ significantly on

adjustment.

* Male diabetic and non - diabetic subjects did not differ significantly on adjustment

4.8 References

De Groot, M. (2014). Depression and diabetes. In Psychosocial Care for People with Diabetes. Young-Hyman D, Peyrot M, (Eds). Alexandria, VA, *American Diabetes Association, 1–16*

Earp, J. A., Strogatz, D. S., Ory, M. G. (1981). The relationship between stressful life events, social support, and high blood pressure control. Paper presented at the National Conference on High Blood Pressure Control, New York.

Egede, L. E., Zheng, D., Simpson, K. (2002). Comorbid depression is associated with increased health care use and expenditures in individuals with diabetes. *Diabetes Care 25, 464–470*

Gilden, J. L., Hendryx, M., Casia, C., Singh, S. P. (1989). The effectiveness of diabetes education programs for older patients and their spouses. *Journal of the American Geriatric Society, 37, 1023–1030.*

Katz, A. M. (1969). Wives of diabetic men. Bull Menninger Clinic, 33, 279-94.

Klausner, E. J., Koenigsberg, H. W., Skolnick, N. (1995). Perceived familial criticism and glucose control in IDDM. International. *Journal of Mental Health, 24, 64–75.*

Outlook, (2014). Innovative collaborations. St. Louis, MO, Washington *University School of Medicine, Spring, 16–17.*

Petroni, F. A. (1969). Significant others and illness behavior: a much neglected sick role contingency. *Sociol Q, 10, 32-41.*

Pollock, S., Christian, B., and Sands, D. (1990). Responses to chronic illness: analysis of psychological and psychological adaptation. *Nursing Research,* 39(5) 300-304.

Schafer, R. B., and Keith, P. M. (1984). A causal analysis of the relationship between the self-concept and marital quality. *J Marriage Fam, 46,* 909-14.

Simmons, S., Ball, S. E. (1984). Marital adjustment and self-actualization in couples married before and after spinal cord injury. *J Marriage Fam, 46, 943-45.*

Singh, C. (2013). An analytic study of death anxiety among type 2 diabetes Mediterranean. *Journal of Social Sciences MCSER Publishing, Rome-Italy.*

Spanier, G. B. (1979). Measuring dyadic adjustment: new scales for assessing the quality of marriage and similar dyads. *J Marriage Fam, 38, 15-28.*

Trief, P. M., Himes, C. L., Orendorff, R., Weinstock, R. S. (2001). The marital relationship and psychosocial adaptation and glycolic control of individuals with diabetes. *Diabetes Care, 23, 1384–1389.*

Trief, P. M., Sandberg, J., Greenberg, R. P. (2003). Describing support: A qualitative study of couples living with diabetes. Families, Systems, & Health, 21, 57–68.

Trief, P. M., Wade, M. J., Britton, K. D., Weinstock, R. S. (2002). A prospective analysis of marital relationship factors and quality of life in diabetes. *Diabetes Care, 25, 1154–1158.*

White, N. E., Richter, J. M., & Fry, C. (1992). Coping, social support, and adaptation to chronic illness. *Western Journal of Nursing Research,* 14(2), 211-224.

Whittemore, R. D., Eramo, T., Melkus, G., & Grey, M. (2005). Metabolic control, self-management and psychosocial adjustment in women with type 2 diabetes. *J Clin Nurs*, 14,195–203.

Willoughby, D. F., Kee, C., Demi, A. (2000). Women's psychosocial adjustment to diabetes. *J, Adv Nurs,* 32, 1422–1430.

Wing, R. R., Marcus, M. D., Epstein, L. H., Jawad, A. A. (1991). A family based approach to the treatment of obese type II diabetic patients. Journal of Consulting and Clinical Psychology, 59,156–162.

CHAPTER – 5

SUMMARY AND CONCLUSIONS

LIST OF CONTENTS

CHAPTER 5

5. Summary and Conclusions

5.1 Introduction

Diabetes a silently killing, currently it is doing billions of dollars of harm to our society, which involves a large amount of innocent citizens oncology patients and millions of others. either as a Type 1 diabetes is long-where the pancreas stops producing insulin or as a result of the patient's body not being able to access the insulin — in a severe long-term illness or all of diabetes — Type 1 diabetes is possible There is growing evidence that suggests a link between lifestyle and rising diabetes rates in the world of the 21st century, but rising levels of obesity are not considered one of equal importance with that of identifying the disease as a global health crisis. As the condition has been described, diabetes is something that develops over time; it takes several alterations in lifestyle to treat and is called the most demanding of all chronic diseases.

Diabetes must be closely controlled by taking medication and exercising every day, because the only way to treat it is to use any of it must be avoided. Because people who suffer from this disorder must undergo dietary adjustments and sometimes struggle with anxiety difficulties, the odds of them having several health conditions are higher. Individuals that are obese are less likely to be satisfied with their lives and are therefore more likely to engage in negative habits including smoking and alcohol and are physically inactive are more likely to be dissatisfied. The new style of life which is prevalent in the world's largest cities and has since been incorporated into the developing cities and metros has been referred to as the global style of urban life, while citizens all of the above cities/cities adhere to this today have only to a portion of its features.

Unfortunately, diabetes has a major impact on the life of many people, and the possibility that people with diabetes can have a worse quality of life is enough for others to consider preventing it when such long-term diseases such as obesity, sleep apnea, heart disease, and kidney disease coexist with diabetes, their symptoms are intensified. Owing to developing diabetes, there is an approximately twofold rise in the chances of fear, shifts in diet, and other challenges twice the chance of marriage issues. In order to survive, people must detect the danger and avoid or decline into a state of unawareness. Under that scenario, the body's anatomy is greatly expands. Problems follow, and certain essential organs are impacted. There is a significant disparity between the demands and the country has on the three relevant to science, schooling, and health care, for Indian citizens for additional treatment.

5.2 Concept of Diabetes

Many people who are going blind, in part due to diabetes, billions who have lost their sight due to diabetes around the world today are in addition to a potentially deadly illness. Often, people who have the illness of job burn will go through all the physical symptoms of cancer before being diagnosed. In these cases, job burn is as fatal as the disease if not identified. Gelatinous retinopathy, formerly known as retinopathy of gelatinous, is an exceedingly common condition that usually causes severe vision loss in both eyes and an unusually rapid breakdown of the skin and blood vessels. Diabetes is a lack of self-control over insulin levels, which is marked by a siphon. There is another expression that describes diabetes, "non-insulin-dependent" or "no-need-for-for-insulin-sugar diabetes". "Non-insulin-dependent" describes it as the disease of having the property of becoming no diabetic under which the urine is free of sugar. There was the first known account of diabetes, which appeared in 1550 B.C.C. It tells about a condition that led a patient to lose weight easily and regularly as well as having trouble urinating. Diabetes has been perceived for 2,000 years as a lethal and crippling illness for the past 2,000 years. Diabetes, also being a form a Greek word meaning "to destroy", was given the Latin name "sues" (or Cynic form of it) after its discoverer, "Aerates, and referred to as a disease which degrades the patient's entire body over time. For fluids linger in the body just to get from place to place; they never carry it for their final dwelling. An average human lifetime may be roughly a century, say, but not usually, decades long. Though it can be excruciating for them, they stand beside you, urination is also easy. Because no vital component of the drink is consumed, the fluid is mostly consists of flesh, much of the drink is eliminated in the urine.

5.3 Meaning of Quality of Life

Quality of life, the degree to which an individual is healthy, comfortable, and able to participate in or enjoy life events. The term *quality of life* is inherently ambiguous, as it can refer both to the experience an individual has of his or her own life and to the living conditions in which individuals find themselves. Hence, quality of life is highly subjective. Whereas one person may define quality of life according to wealth or satisfaction with life, another person may define it in terms of capabilities (e.g., having the ability to live a good life in terms of emotional and physical well-being). A disabled person may report a high quality of life, whereas a healthy person who recently lost a job may report a low quality of life. Within the arena of health care, quality of life is viewed as multidimensional, encompassing emotional, physical, material, and social well-being.

5.4 Definition of Mental Health

Mental health refers to cognitive, behavioral, and emotional well-being. It is all about how people think, feel, and behave. People sometimes use the term "mental health" to mean the absence of a mental disorder. Mental health can affect daily living, relationships, and physical health.

According to WHO "Mental health is a state of well-being in which an individual realizes his or her own abilities, can cope with the normal stresses of life, can work productively, and is able to make a contribution to his or her community."

The WHO stress that mental health is "more than just the absence of mental disorders or disabilities." Peak mental health is about not only avoiding active conditions but also looking after ongoing wellness and happiness.

5.5 Meaning and Definition of Marital Adjustment

Marital adjustment can be defined as the mental state among couples in which there is an overall feeling of happiness and satisfaction with their marriage. It, therefore, calls for experiencing a satisfactory relationship between spouses characterized by mutual concern, care, understanding, and acceptance. All the marriages are aimed at happiness in one or another way. Most couples become married filled up with expectations. Some of

the expectations will be realistic while others are unrealistic. This is due to the complex nature of marriage and each individual is as complex as a universe. Therefore, in marriage two universes come together. Happiness, satisfaction, and fulfilment of expectations are possible only by mutual adjustments that lead to a common concept of marriage. Carl Rogers (1972) views this concept of marriage as the basis of many marital adjustments. He speaks about two main concepts of marriage: ...for some it (marriage) is a romantic box...a tight fence, limiting freedom, ... roomy comfortable box.... a magic box, resolving the difficulties in their relationship...'. for some, ' it is an exciting exploration of new avenues... each is given freedom and encouragement to develop full potential. If both parties perceive accurately and understand clearly their concept of marriage, things go smoothly and good understanding takes place. When there are differences in their concept and perception, problems are likely to occur. The major role transition between couples in values, attitudes, and beliefs when they start living together is one of the major causes of marital adjustment issues. Spouses enter marriage relationships with different beliefs about happiness and they differ in their expectations of happiness too. Therefore, mutual communication and sharing are the backbones for adjustment in marriage.

5.6 Definition of Life Satisfaction

Life-satisfaction is the degree to which a person positively evaluates the overall quality of his/her life as-a whole. In other words, how much the person likes the life he/she leads (Veenhoven, 1996) Donovan& Halpern(2002) discuss -minded and creative in their thinking. In Furthermore, people who are satisfied with their lives tend to be healthier and life satisfaction is inversely related to turnover intent (Donovan & Halpern, 2002; Lambert *et al.*, 2009).

Life satisfaction has been one of the oldest and most persistently investigated issues in the study of adulthood (Lewis & Borders, 1995). Life satisfaction refers to an assessment of the overall conditions of existence as derived

5.7 Concept of Adjustment

Adjustment is a behavioural process by which a person maintains balance among various needs that one encounters at a given point of time. Each and every situation of life demands that the person concerned should be able to effectively perform in accordance with some guiding principles and should be able to strike a balance among various forces. Adjustment is defined as a process wherein one builds variations in the behaviour to achieve harmony with oneself, others or the environment with an aim to maintain the state of equilibrium between the individual and the environment.

Adjustment has been analyzed as an achievement as well as a process in psychology. Interpreting adjustment as an achievement would necessitate effective performance in doing what one was expected to and engaged in. This would mean judging the quality on certain parameters. However, psychologists have been interested to examine adjustment as a process. This entails examining the interaction of the individual with the external world.

If the relationship between the individual and his/ her environment is in accordance with the norms then the adjustment is achieved. The behaviour of the person concerned would be considered normal. Gross deviation from the norms demand clinical investigations and interventions. Such deviations are defined as maladjustment. Severe deviations can be classified as abnormal behaviour.

5.8 Methodology

5.8.1 Objectives

The objectives of the present research were as follows:

- To measure the impact of diabetes on mental health.
- To measure the impact of diabetes on marital adjustment.
- To measure the impact of diabetes on life satisfaction.
- To measure the impact of diabetes on adjustment.
- To measure the impact of diabetes on death anxiety.

5.8.2 Hypotheses

On the basis of abovementioned objectives following hypotheses were formulated:

- The mental health of non – diabetic subjects will be better than diabetic subjects.
- The marital adjustment of non – diabetic subjects will be better than diabetic subjects.
- The life satisfaction of diabetic subjects will not be better than non - diabetic subjects.
- The adjustment of non - diabetic subjects will be better than diabetic subjects.
- The death anxiety of diabetic subjects will be higher than non - diabetic subjects.

5.8.3 Sample

The sample of the present study consisted of 100 diabetic and 100non - diabetic subjects (age group of 20 - 55 years) residing in Hazaribagh, Ramgarh and Ranchi district. These Data was selected by stratified random technique. The stratification was based on 2 factors of gender (male and female), and 2 factors of health status (diabetic and non - diabetic). Therefore, the research design was based on 2 x 2 factorial design and factors of stratification were:

- **Gender** **2 :** Male and Female
- **Health Status - 2 : Diabetic** and Non - Diabetic

There were 4 strata. From each stratum, 50 cases were selected randomly making a total of 200 cases.

5.8.4 Process of Sample Selection

Firstly subjects were contacted personally and briefed about the purpose of the study. Informed consent was taken prior to the administration of tools. Then participants were given the questionnaires and proper instructions for completing the questionnaires. On the fixed date, all scales were used into two sessions. In session I, Personal Data Questionnaire,PGIHealth Questionnaire and Death Anxiety Scale were administered on Diabetic and non- diabetic subjects, while in session II Life Satisfaction Scale, Mohsin-Shamshad Adjustment Inventory and Marital Adjustment Questionnairewere administered on Diabetic and non- diabetic subjects.

5.8.5 Tools used in the Data Collection

The following tools used for the data collection:

- Personal Data Questionnaire (PDQ)
- PGI Health Questionnaire (PGI HQ)
- Marital Adjustment Questionnaire (MAQ)
- Life Satisfaction Scale (LSS)
- Mohsin - Shamshad Adjustment Inventory (MSAI)
- Death Anxiety Scale (DAS)

➢ Personal Data Questionnaire (PDQ)

Personal Data Questionnaire was prepared by the researcher. This elicited respondent's basic information, such as name, age, gender, level of education, place of residence etc.

➢ PGI Health Questionnaire (PGI HQ)

This questionnaire was developed by Verma, Wig & Prasad (1985). This test is useful not only for clinical work in screening and assessing the progress of treatment but has a larger utility in clinical psychiatric research. It is a short, simple test with low difficulty value for items and it can be used with illiterate, unsophisticated population also. Higher score usually indicates greater chances of developing psychiatric symptoms.

Reliability: Reliability of the test was examined using 'test-retest' and 'split-half' method and was found to be significantly high (0.88 & 0.86respectively).

Validity: Validity of PGI HQ N-1 was established administering other well-known test of neuroticism concomitantly. It was found that the total score of the PGI HQ N-1 was highly correlates with similar traits of other scale. Separate scores of section "A" and "B" were found relatively lower correlation (though still significant) with measures of neuroticism onother tests. This confirms that a combined of physical and psychological scores constitutes a better measure of neuroticism. If one obtains high scores only on one of the two sections, then there are relatively less chances of his being a case of neurosis. The test was cross validated on fresh sample from Chandigarh. Ahmadabad and Rohtak. It was found that mean scores of male &female psychiatric patients were comparable but were comparable but were markedly distinct from normal.

➢ Marital Adjustment Questionnaire (MAQ)

This questionnaire was developed by Pramod Kumar and Kanchana Rohatgi. This was used to access the marital adjustment among the married couples. This questionnaire consists of 25 items, out of which 22 items are positive and 3 items are negative. There are two response alternatives for each item: Yes and No. for positive items, score is 1 and 0 is given respectively and vice-versa for the negative items. Negatives items are 4, 10, and 19. Except these three items all are positive items. The sum of all 25 items gives overall marital adjustment scores. Thus range of scores is 0 to 25. Higher scores, shows better the marital adjustment and vice-versa. Reliability of this scale is 0.75 and validity is reported 0.78.

➢ Life Satisfaction Scale (LSS)

This scale was designed and developed byQ.G. Alam& Dr. Ramji Srivastava (2001). Published by National psychological corporation, Agra. The L.S.S. comprises of 60 items related to six areas of life viz. Health, Personal, Economic, Marital, Social and Job. The responses are to given in yes/no. yes responses indicate Satisfaction, whereas No indicate Dissatisfaction.

Test-Retest reliability quotient is 0.84. The validity of the scale was obtained by correlating it with Saxon's Adjustment Inventory and Srivastaava adjustment inventory. The quotient obtained was 0.74and 0.84 respectively.

➢ Mohsin - Shamshad Adjustment Inventory (MSAI)

This inventory was used to measure the adjustment of the subject. It is Hindi adaptation of bell adjustment inventory. It was modified in 1987.This inventory is consists of 124 items, which measure adjustment, four dimension namely, Home, health, social and emotional.

The reliability of this scale is .75 to .89 and the validity of the scale is .58 to .89.

➢ Death Anxiety Scale

This scale was developed by G.P. Thakur and Manju Thakur (1983). This scale had sixteen statements. Statement numbers, 1, 2, 4, 5, 7, 9, 10, 12, 13, 15 and 16 were positively worded and numbers 3, 6, 8, 11 and 14 were negatively worded. Responses on the positively worded statement would get 5, 4, 3, 2 and 1 for the "quite true", "true", "Undecided", "false" and "quite true", "true", "Undecided", "false" and "quite false" response categories. The maximum score, one could get on the scale, would be 80 and the minimum would be 16.

Reliability:

The death anxiety scale was administered on a sample of 206 Indians of both the sexes for ascertaining reliability co-efficient. Internal consistency reliability co-efficient using Kuder-Richardson formula was found to be 0.78 and a test retest reliability co-efficient with a gap of about twelve weeks on 65 Ss was 0.86. The reliability co-efficient, therefore, were considered satisfactory.

Validity:

With a view to ascertaining validity co-efficient of the death anxiety scale, the scale along with the Templar's scale of the CPS, there scales-Trust (T), Activity (A) and Extroversion (E) had negative relationship with the Thakur Death anxiety scale (TDAS). Other five scale - orderliness (O), Social conformity (C), emotional stability (S), Masculinity (M) and Empathy (P) had positive relationship with the TDAS in greater or smaller degree.

5.9 Results and Discussion

The data of present study is analyzed and reported in this chapter. The results are presented under the following points:

5.9.1 The impact of diabetes on mental health.

5.9.2 The impact of diabetes on marital adjustment.

5.9.3 The impact of diabetes on life satisfaction.

5.9.4 The impact of diabetes on adjustment.

5.9.5 The impact of diabetes on death anxiety.

5.9.1 Impact of Diabetes on Mental Health

- Diabetic subjects were significantly high mental health than non-diabetic subjects.
- Male diabetic subjects were significantly high mental health than male non-diabetic subjects.
- Female diabetic subjects were significantly high mental health than female non-diabetic subjects.

5.9.2 The Impact of Diabetes on Death Anxiety

- Diabetic and non- diabetic subjects did not differ significantly on death anxiety.
- Male diabetic and non - diabetic subjects did not differ significantly on death anxiety.
- Female diabetic subjects were significantly high death anxiety than female non adjustment.-diabetic subjects.

5.9.3 The Impact of Diabetes on Life Satisfaction

- Diabetic and non - diabetic subjects did not differ significantly on life satisfaction.
- Male diabetic and non - diabetic subjects did not differ significantly on life satisfaction.
- Female diabetic and non - diabetic subjects did not differ significantly on

5.9.4 The Impact of Diabetes on Adjustment

- Diabetic and non - diabetic subjects did not differ significantly on adjustment.
- Male diabetic and non - diabetic subjects did not differ significantly on adjustment.
- Female diabetic subjects were significantly high adjustment than female non-diabetic subjects.

5.9.5 The Impact of Diabetes on Marital Adjustment

- Diabetic subjects were significantly high marital adjustment than non-diabetic subjects.
- diabetic subjects were significantly high marital adjustment than male non-diabetic subjects.
- female diabetic subjects were significantly high marital adjustment than female non-diabetic subjects.

5.10 Critique of the Present Research

This research was undertaken to study the impact of diabetes on mental health, marital adjustment, life satisfaction, adjustment and death anxiety among subjects of Hazaribagh, Ramgarh and Ranchi district. The merits, limitation, and recommendation of the present research are as follows:

5.10.1 Merits of the Present Research

The merits of the present research are as follows:

- The study was empirical and scientific statistical methods were used to analyze the data.
- The present research explored the impact of diabetes on mental health, marital adjustment, life satisfaction, adjustment and death anxiety among subjects of Hazaribagh, Ramgarh and Ranchi district. There was no study in Jharkhand focusing on the impact of diabetes on mental health, marital adjustment, life satisfaction, adjustment and death anxiety among subjects of Ranchi, Hazaribagh and Ramgarh district. The present research has filled up this gap.

5.10.2 Limitations of the Present Research

The limitations of the present research can be listed as under:

- The study was conducted only on 200subjects. Results of the present study may not be generalized.
- The data was collected by using survey method which can't work for its depth exploration. Hence the projective and interview method might be the suitable method in order to know the impact of diabetes on mental health, marital adjustment, life satisfaction, adjustment and death anxiety.

- The present research has been done by taking the sample from Ranchi, Ramgarh and Hazaribagh districts. Sample from other districts hould be taken for better knowledge.

5.10.3 Implications of the Present Research

- The research has explored the impact of diabetes on marital adjustment. Which may help diabetic married couples to make their marital adjustment better.
- The research has explored the impact of diabetes on life satisfaction. Which helps family counselors to make program for improving the life satisfaction of diabetic married couples.
- The findings of present study will help to understand how diabetes impacts on death anxiety and mental health. Which help us to increase the diabetic married couple's life satisfaction and mental health related programs and their planning.

5.10.4 Recommendations of the Present Research

On the basis of findings of the present research, recommendations can be listed as follow:

- Projective method with diabetic subjects may provide a more comprehensive understanding of impact of diabetes on mental health, marital adjustment, life satisfaction, adjustment and death anxiety.
- The research should be done on large sample groups, taking more variables; socioeconomic status, scheduled tribe, tribes, different age groups and different educational levels.
- The data should be collected qualitatively. In order to enrich the qualitative data other methods, such as case study, focus group discussion etc. should be used.
- Interview method with may provide a more comprehensive understanding of impact of diabetes on mental health, marital adjustment, life satisfaction, adjustment and death anxiety.

5.11 Main Findings

- Diabetic subjects had significantly high mental health than non-diabetic subjects.
- Male diabetic subjects had significantly high mental health than male non diabeticsubjects.
- Female diabetic subjects had significantly high mental health than female nondiabetic subjects.
- Diabetic and non- diabetic subjects did not differ significantly on death anxiety.
- Male diabetic and non - diabetic subjects did not differ significantly on deathanxiety.
- Female diabetic subjects had significantly high death anxiety than female nondiabetic subjects.
- Diabetic and non - diabetic subjects did not differ significantly on life satisfaction.
- Male diabetic and non - diabetic subjects did not differ significantly on lifesatisfaction.
- Female diabetic and non - diabetic subjects did not differ significantly on lifesatisfaction.
- Diabetic and non - diabetic subjects did not differ significantly on adjustment.
- Male diabetic and non - diabetic subjects did not differ significantly on adjustment

5.12 References

Donovan, N., & Halpern, D. (2002). Life satisfaction: the state of knowledge and implications for government. Retrieved online on Sep 12, 2011fromhttp://www.cabinetoffice.gov.uk/media/cabinetoffice/strategy/assets/paper.pdf.

Lambert, E. G., Hogan, N. L., Elechi, O. O., Jiang, S., Laux, J. M., Dupuy, P. & Morris, A. (2009). A further examination of antecedents of correctional staff life satisfaction. *The Social Science Journal,* 46, 689-706.

Lewis, V., & Borders, L. (1995). Life satisfaction of single middle-aged professional women. *Journal of Counselling and Development,* 74, 94-100.

Veenhoven, R. (1996). The study of life satisfaction. In W.E.Saris, R. Veenhoven, A.C. Scherpenzeel, & B. Bunting (Eds.), *A comparative study of satisfaction with life in Europe* (pp.11-48). Budapest: Eotvos University Press.

Recommendation:

The findings of this research indicates that diabetic and non-diabetic persons vary on mental health of the authority wants to harness the capacity of diabetic person, their mental health should be alleviated only then diabetic patient will provide best service to nation. Furthermore impact of gender is also important factor in utilizing the potentialities of diabetic patient become mental health of female patient is much affected by diabetes. If government wants to utilize the potentiality of women diabetic, then mental health must be sound.

It is also found that diabetic persons have high death anxiety than non-diabetic persons. So, diabetic patient should not be allocated risky job where they cannot work. It is also noticed that diabetic and non-diabetes are not different on life satisfaction. It means if both types of people are employed, then will no deference in life satisfaction of employee. No effect is made to alleviate their life satisfaction. Both type of patient will be equal in life satisfaction

Future work:

This work will lead to different new research which may be summarized as:

1. Future work may involve like emotional competence, ego strength, ego involvement etc.
2. The next research may assess the impact of next other disease like Hypertension, peptic ulcer and family problem.
3. The future work may involve different age group.
4. The next future research may involve different ethnic group.
5. The next future research may be done on impact of coronary heart problem.

Conclusion :

This works can be concluded as follows

Diabetic subjects has high mental health than non-diabetic subjects. Male diabetic subjects has high mental health than male non diabetic subjects. Female diabetic subjects had better mental health than female non- diabetic subjects. Diabetic and non- diabetic subjects do not differ on death anxiety. Male diabetic and non – diabetic did not differ on death anxiety. Female diabetic and non-diabetic are different on death anxiety. Future work It is also observed that male diabetic and non- diabetic are not different on life Satisfaction. female diabetic and non- Diabetic are not different on life Satisfaction . it is also observed that Diabetic and non- Diabetic are different on martial adjustment. Diabetic and non-Diabetic subject are different on marital adjustment. Last it is also observed that diabetics female and non- Diabetic female and not different on marital adjustment

Future finding:

- Projective method with diabetic subjects may provide a more comprehensive understanding of impact of diabetes on mental health, marital adjustment, life satisfaction, adjustment and death anxiety.
- The research should be done on large sample groups, taking more variables; socioeconomic status, scheduled tribe, tribes, different age groups and different educational levels.
- The data should be collected qualitatively. In order to enrich the qualitative data other methods, such as case study, focus group discussion etc. should be used.
- Interview method with may provide a more comprehensive understanding of impact of diabetes on mental health, marital adjustment, life satisfaction, adjustment and death anxiety.

Total no, of references used – 18

Total no of page of thesis - 203

Tital of the thesis **Measuring Impact of Diabetes On Quality of life**

CPSIA information can be obtained
at www.ICGtesting.com
Printed in the USA
BVHW072145290123
657301BV00009B/1015

9 781805 454717